NO SHORTCUTS

NO SHORTCUTS
What it Really Takes

AMJAD JABER

NO WAY BUT THROUGH
NWBT

Contents

From the Trenches of Life

I wasn't born into any of this.
Not leadership.
Not privilege.
Not even the language of this book.

At almost sixteen, I got a lucky break, I immigrated to the United States with my siblings. No parents, just four kids with green cards and a chance at a new life. For the first time, we had a place to belong, a path to walk, a system to join.

My parents couldn't come. Finances decided that.
They stayed behind, worked honest jobs, and sent every dollar to give us more than they had. Their directive wasn't pressure; it was a lifeline:

Learn English. Finish school. Master honest skills. Stay current with technology. Live with integrity.

Back then, I thought they were giving us tools for survival.

Now I see they were preparing us for a world that doesn't always reward effort. A world that often confuses noise for substance, exploitation for strength, kindness for weakness.

They didn't try to shield us.

They prepared us, with a mindset that became my edge.
Maybe my only one.

You have an edge too, even if it's buried under doubt or drift.
This book, *No Shortcuts: What It Really Takes*, is about sharpening that edge.

The title is heavy because there are no shortcuts, and what it really takes is more than most people carry.

I'm not here to preach, I'm here to share what has worked for me, consistently and in the parts of my life that held when everything else shook.

But let me set the record straight: *I'm not the model of discipline.*

I start some mornings without intention or direction. I break routines. I still carry vices I am not proud of. Some I try to outwork, ignore, or sometimes bury. I also drift, flinch, and chase comfort when I know better. And I know you do too.

I've helped the wrong people, ignored the right ones, and hurt others through action or neglect.

I've stayed silent when I should've spoken up, acted for attention when it wasn't necessary, and let emotions override judgment, calling it "passion," to dodge the deeper inner work.

I will say this: Every time I faced those mistakes, without excuses, my Code sharpened.

It didn't become louder.
Not cleaner.
Just clearer.

My effort started feeling like alignment and stopped feeling like struggle.

I've learned that even good virtues can shift into bad ones, into extremes, into overuse.

This Code helped me find the right balance at the right time. Sometimes it cost me, like walking away from a shady deal or chasing wins that dulled my focus. I'll share these stories as we move ahead.

The Code will help you, too.

To be clear, I didn't always face it alone. Sometimes the cost broke through my denial. Other times, people I love pulled me aside and had to set me straight. I pushed some away, but I've learned something very important:

Real growth comes from deep inner work but only after you let in the right voices. The ones offering hard, clean truth. Not insecurities dressed as advice.

> *I've listened to both*
> *I've rejected both.*
> *And I've paid for both.*
> *That's how I got tougher.*

There are parts of my life I did right:
In my work and close relationships, I showed up. Still do.
With consistency, weight, and a lot of heart.

I held the line when it was easier to let it slide.
I didn't shortcut my work or my bonds. Those are still sacred to me.

And those areas have become my strongest, not by luck, but by a Code I lived; even when I stumbled elsewhere.

I traced what set them apart:
A mindset I never named. Until now.

This book isn't a manual. It's not a highlight reel.
It's that Code.

Forged in failure.
Sharpened by choice.
Tested under weight.

I wish I'd applied it sooner. Not just to work and relationships, but to health, habits, money, and time.

When I didn't apply it, I drifted, and paid a heavy price for it, quietly, and over years.

I have lived both ways.
Without the Code, I faltered.
With it, I excelled.

So I write this from the trenches, not the mountaintop.
I'm proof the Code works when you hold it.
And proof life catches up when you don't.

In these pages, I'll share my stories, mistakes and all to show you how I learned.

You'll learn to carry this Code.
Step by step.
Through a mindset you already have.

You don't need perfection.
Just clarity when it counts.

If you're tired of drifting, chasing, or carrying weight without a frame, this is your reset.

A way to lead with something real under your feet.

There's no cheating. **No shortcuts.**
Only one way forward: **No way but through.**

CHAPTER ONE

Before You Begin

THE FIRST RECEIPT

The first time I remember trying to take a shortcut, I was about twelve.

I had fallen at school and needed stitches. The school called my dad to pick me up and take me to the hospital. After it was all done, my dad told me something that made my day:
"If you go back inside and get the receipt from the hospital, we'll submit it to the school's insurance. And if they pay us back, you get to keep the money."

It was around forty dollars, more than three months' worth of my daily allowance. I was thrilled.

So I went back in and got the receipt. Only they gave me two. Different dates. Same visit. Same total.

To me, that meant double the money. I walked out grinning, got into the car, and told my dad, "They made a mistake and I'm going to get eighty bucks!"

He didn't smile. He asked to see the receipts.
Without saying a word, he tore both of them in half.
And then he slapped me.

It was the only time my dad ever hit me.
And what he said next never left me:
"We have lived our whole lives honestly and you want to start yours by lying and cheating?"

That moment branded something deep into me. That slap wasn't about money. It was about protecting who I would have become if he had let it slide. And I didn't need a second lesson after that.

WHEN THE PRICE WAS HIGHER

Years later, the stakes were a lot bigger.
That's when the second shortcut came dressed as opportunity.

It was a deal overseas. Would've made me rich overnight.
It was dirty. Obvious. Fast. And I didn't have money.

I didn't argue. Didn't negotiate. Just said, "Let me check with my boss."

Let's be clear, I never checked with my boss. But I remembered that slap from my dad.

Forty-eight hours later, I was on a flight back to the U.S.
Not proud. Not sure if I'd done the right thing. Just gone.

Years later and in hindsight everyone that was going to be part of this deal was either killed or incarcerated.

That day didn't create my Standard. It revealed it. I had never cheated on small things. Not when no one was watching. Not when it was easy to justify.

But that moment sharpened something. This wasn't about policy or consequences. It was about what I was willing to build my life on, and what I wasn't.

And I thought once you passed a test like that, you were good. Safe. Clean. Unshakeable.

I was wrong.

DRIFT DOESN'T START LOUD

Years later, after real success, after I had built something clean, the shortcuts came back. Not through backdoor deals or shady handshakes, but quietly, through a screen.

I STARTED TRADING OPTIONS.

At first, it felt harmless. Temporary. Something I did on the side, just for myself. I told myself it was personal, that it wouldn't touch the business, the team, or the real work.

But I was lying to myself.

It didn't start with a big loss. It started with distraction—checking trades during meetings, watching price swings instead of watching the people who depended on me. My focus scattered, and I kept telling myself I had it under control.

The truth was, I didn't.

I wasn't doing anything illegal. I wasn't breaking rules. But I was off course. The sharpness that used to define my work had started to slip. Conversations felt flatter. Work moved slower. And rest, even when I tried, didn't restore me like it used to.

I kept pretending the damage was contained, just numbers on a screen, just a personal habit. But shortcuts don't stay in their lanes. They bleed. And in the end, it wasn't the market that woke me up.

It was the drift.

The slow erosion of clarity. The quiet separation between who I was and how I was moving and the realization that I hadn't noticed until it was already happening.

THE INTERVENTION

It was my business partner who pulled me aside.

No judgment. No panic. Just presence.
He didn't question the money. He questioned me.
Calm and clear, he reminded me who I was before this. What we had built. And how easy it is to forget what you've spent years becoming.

That conversation hit harder than any market loss.
I couldn't defend it.

- I had drifted.
- So I shut it down.
- Took the loss.

And returned to what always worked:
Quiet choices. Hard ones. Stacked again, day by day—until clarity came back.

WHAT THE DRIFT TAUGHT ME

Shortcuts don't always show up dirty, they show up disguised as efficiency.
The real cost of a shortcut isn't the money, it's your sharpness.

Integrity isn't a moment. It's a rhythm. Discipline isn't rigid. It's rooted.

The people who hold you to your Standard are the ones who care the most.

BEFORE YOU BEGIN

What I will share with you isn't a motivational speech.
Not a list of hacks.
Not a promise that hard work alone will save you.
It's something quieter and stronger.

This is for the one who's carried more than they let on.
The one who shows up, solves problems, who holds the line and still wonders if anyone sees it.
The one who's led without applause, recovered in silence, and kept moving even when the road felt thankless.

It's for the person who's done everything right and still got passed over.
Who's watched others take shortcuts and get ahead.
Who's wondered if the game is rigged or if doing it the right way even works anymore.

Here's the truth:

Some people start the race halfway down the track.
Some get credit without showing up.
Some trip others just to win. And some build the whole darn track.
But that doesn't have to be the story.

Because there is a way forward.
Not a shortcut. Not a trick. **A Standard.**

One that sharpens under pressure.
One that guides when the noise gets loud.
One that holds when no one's watching.

That's what this book is for.

> *It won't give you confidence.*
> *It won't hand you discipline.*
> *It won't promise success just because you showed up.*

But it will give you a Code to carry. A framework that holds up under pressure. A way to stop drifting and start leading—without needing a title to do it.

This is not a repackaged speech dressed up as a chapter.
It's something else entirely.

It's a Code.

A way of carrying yourself that works when things are calm and holds when everything breaks loose.

And it's not made for one type of person.
It's not just for the tough, the experienced, the confident, or the polished.

It's for anyone, I mean anyone with the will to do better, but who's been waiting for a direction that makes sense.

If you're tired of reacting,
Tired of wondering if you're doing it right,
Tired of chasing progress with no compass,

This is your starting point.

And if you want to start, then here's what you need to know:

> *You can't control the market.*
> *You can't control your past.*
> *You can't control the politics at work or the system you inherited.*
> *You can't control who your parents are.*
> *You can't control the society you grew up within.*

There is a long list of things you can't control.

But you **can** control your ***conviction.***
You can control how you lead, especially when it's hard.

And conviction isn't a feeling.

Belief isn't a feeling, it's a decision.

But that decision needs something solid to stand on.

That's what this book gives you: **A foundation.**

Not theory. Not fluff. Not slogans.
What's in this book has been field-tested.
In pressure. In silence. In failure. In real life.
And it holds.

Because it's built from principles so clear and so consistent they start to run in the background.

> *They become your default under pressure.*
> *They shape your tone.*
> *They power your response.*
> *They guide your recovery.*

And over time, quietly, steadily; they change you.
You get clearer.
You get sharper.
You become more useful, more reliable, more respected.
More you.

And the beauty of it?

This Standard works everywhere.

> *You can lead a shift.*
> *Raise a daughter.*
> *Run a company.*
> *Or rebuild yourself.*

You don't need a title to carry weight.
You just need a Standard that holds.

What's in this book gives you the tools to do that.
To move with intention instead of instinct.

To lead without waiting for permission.
To stand for something when it's easier to stay silent.

You won't wake up great.
But you can build it quietly, over time, piece by piece.
By stacking small decisions that matter.
By staying true to your Code when no one's looking.
By showing up, for others, and for yourself.

And one day maybe five years from now, maybe fifty,
you'll look back and realize:

You didn't wing it.
You didn't fake it.
You didn't follow the noise.

You led your life with intention.
You ran on a Standard.
You carried the weight.

And because of that, you became someone worth following.

So if you're ready. Not to be perfect, but to be better.
Not to impress anyone, but to be someone.

Then turn the page.

This won't be easy.
But it will be worth it.

Let's get to work

CHAPTER TWO

The Custodian Standard

SECTION 1: WHAT THEY DON'T TEACH YOU ABOUT LEADERSHIP

The perception of leadership today is loud. Fast. Built for the feed.

But real leadership doesn't shout.
It doesn't chase the spotlight or perform for approval.
It holds steady, quietly, when no one's watching.

Because trust isn't earned through noise.
And legacy isn't built on momentum.
It's built on consistency, when no one's clapping, and the cameras are gone.

Sometimes I've been the loud one.
I've raised my voice in rooms I should've walked out of.
Spoken too fast when I should've let silence do the work.

Almost every time I've led with volume, I've regretted it.
Not because I lost control, but because I lost clarity.

And then there are times I go completely quiet.
So deep in thought that I zone out, staring at the ceiling, rubbing my head, not saying a word. It's not nerves. It's pressure moving through calculation.

In those moments, I'm not detached, I'm completely locked in.
I'm measuring what it's going to cost from every angle.

It took me years to understand both sides of that swing.
The urge to speak fast when I feel challenged.
The instinct to go quiet when the stakes are heavy.

But leadership doesn't live in either extreme.
It lives in restraint.
In presence.
In knowing when to speak and when to lead without saying a
word.

It's not about the loudest person in the room.
It's about the one who holds steady when the noise fades.
The one who protects what matters when no one's watching.

That's where real leadership lives.
Not in performance. Not in ego.
But in the quiet moments that test the Standard.

Custodians don't need permission to lead this way.
They don't need applause.
They just need a line they refuse to cross and the conviction to
hold it.

Because even when the road doesn't allow for the long way,
there's always a right way to carry the moment.

SECTION 2: THE CUSTODIAN AND EXPLOITER MINDSETS

Most people don't live inside just one mindset.
They move between them depending on pressure, energy, and
cost.

But two patterns show up again and again:

The Custodian Mindset

- Sees leadership as stewardship.
- Asks: *What's been entrusted? What needs to be protected? Even if no one's watching.*
- Moves with care, even when no one is measuring.
- Carries the Standard, even when it's inconvenient.

The Custodian mindset doesn't always look impressive. In fact, at first glance, it often looks slow. Tiring. Inefficient. Like someone taking the long road when faster options are available. It looks like overthinking when others are already moving. Like being too careful. Too stubborn. Too invested.

It won't get applause right away, because it doesn't perform. It doesn't chase optics. It delays reward to protect what lasts.

And sometimes, it will be mistaken for weakness. You'll hear:

"You're not moving fast enough."
"You're overcomplicating."
"You're holding the bar too high."

And in those moments, it'll take everything in you to stay the course.

But that's the quiet strength of the Custodian: they aren't fueled by speed. They're anchored by purpose. And while the Exploiter might win first, the Custodian builds what outlasts them both.

The Exploiter Mindset

- Sees leadership as opportunity.
- Asks: *What can be gained? How much can be extracted with the least resistance?*
- Moves for speed, comfort, or personal advantage.
- Leaves responsibility behind when it becomes heavy.

The danger of the Exploiter mindset is that it doesn't always show up looking ugly. Sometimes it shows up looking sharp. Productive. Efficient. Respected. You might see it in someone who knows how to win fast, who says all the right things in meetings, who delivers numbers—but leaves trust bleeding everywhere they go.

And if we're being honest, most of us don't spot it in ourselves when it starts. It doesn't announce itself with a moral collapse. It starts smaller. We justify skipping hard conversations because they're uncomfortable. We shift weight onto someone else's back because we're too tired to carry it ourselves. We move faster than we should, because the win looks close and we think we deserve it.

That's the real danger: the Exploiter doesn't always feel like a villain. Sometimes it feels like momentum.

But it erodes everything if left unchecked—teams, cultures, reputations, and standards. It rewards ease, not endurance. And the longer it runs unchallenged, the more it rewires your instincts away from stewardship and toward self-preservation.

Neither mindset is permanent.
Both live inside each of us.

The Custodian in You

You weren't missing anything.
You weren't broken.
You were just distracted, buried under noise, urgency, and the race to survive.

It's not given by titles.
It's not granted by systems.
It's carried by those who decide it matters enough to protect.

You don't need permission to move toward it.
You don't need a perfect history to qualify for it.
You don't need anyone to crown you.

You just need to remember what you already carry
and choose to build with it.

Patience will strengthen it.
Discipline will sharpen it.
Endurance will carry it through.

Custodians aren't manufactured. They're forged.
And they're remembered; one decision, one act of stewardship,
one moment of courage at a time.

This path isn't about who you were.
It's about what you choose next.

The door is open.
Step forward.

SECTION 3: WHAT CUSTODIANS REALLY LOOK LIKE

Custodians aren't defined by title.
They're defined by what they choose to carry.

And they exist everywhere; leading quietly, often overlooked, in
ways few expect:

Through integrity at work

- A nurse who doesn't clock out until she hands off her patients
  fully because life deserves more than a checklist.
- A cashier who reports a double refund that no one else caught
  because stealing is still stealing, even when it's untraceable.

- A factory worker who pauses production for ten minutes because the equipment doesn't sound right and refuses to pass risk downstream.
- A software engineer who doesn't pad the hours, even when they easily could because someone trusted their honesty.
- A small business owner who pays his crew before paying himself because the job isn't done until the team is taken care of.

By exercising moral restraint

- A teacher who holds the line on grading not because it's easy, but because inflating scores robs her students of growth.
- A mother who refuses to lie on school forms to get her kid an advantage because the truth matters more than coming out ahead.
- A high school principal who suspends a star athlete for violating the Code, even when the board pressures him to "just let it go."
- A pastor who turns down a donation meant to buy silence because integrity is not for sale.
- A major donor to the hospital who refuses to use his influence to pressure the board for an earlier surgery date for himself.

By showing quiet courage

- A son who chooses not to yell back at his father, even when he's hurt, because he respects who he is, not how others behave.
- A teen who walks away from his friend group because they mock someone who can't fight back.
- A line-cook who won't send out a bad plate, even if no one notices, because the guest deserves better.

- A waitress who covers a coworker's table during the lunch rush not for tips, but because the customer was about to walk out.

Through everyday leadership

- A grandfather who shows up early to help his neighbor fix a fence because someone once did the same for him.
- A grocery clerk who stops to sweep a spill without being told because someone could get hurt, and she's not passing that forward.
- A bus driver who waits an extra 30 seconds for a running child because she remembers what it felt like to be left behind.
- A young man who deletes a photo he could have shared because someone's dignity matters more than laughs.
- A big sister who lets her little brother sleep in her room because the arguing downstairs makes him scared.

These aren't gestures.
They're not moments of niceness.
They're acts of clarity. Of restraint. Of invisible leadership.

Custodians don't wait to be asked.
They don't need cameras or credit.
They move because something would've broken quietly, slowly, permanently, if they hadn't stepped in.

And that choice, made in silence, is what changes everything.

When Custodians show up, their presence rewires the environment:

- Standards rise.
- Trust settles.
- Clarity returns.

But don't mistake a Custodian's steadiness for softness.

They aren't naive. They know how to guard more than just the work.
They guard the room, the people doing it right.
They guard the tone, the trust, the Standard itself.

And they can spot an Exploiter early. It's the one who shows up for the credit, not the cost.
The one who confuses charm with conviction.
Who dresses up shortcuts as strategy.

Custodians have felt what it's like when someone dodges weight and they don't let that take root.

Because once you've carried something the right way,
you don't stand by while someone else undermines it for convenience.
Not in your name. Not on your watch.

That's what Custodians really look like.

SECTION 4: THE OATH

Some professions require a formal oath—doctors, judges, pilots, public servants.
But real leadership, in any role, needs an internal oath too.

Because without one, you drift.
You start reacting instead of deciding.
You move faster, but with less clarity.
And eventually, you forget what you said you'd never trade.

This isn't a speech.
It's not for applause.
It's a private contract with responsibility itself.

The Custodian Oath

- I will not take shortcuts.
- I will not harm others, intentionally or by neglect.
- I will not trade ethics for speed.
- I will not trade safety for savings.
- I will not trade people for profit.
- I will not chase credit when the weight is mine to carry.
- I will not stay silent when the cost is being passed downstream.
- I will not delay hard decisions just to be liked.
- I will not abandon the Standard to make things easier.
- I will not confuse motion with leadership.
- I will not forget who I serve.
- **And I will correct my course when I drift.**

This isn't about signaling virtue.
It's about staying anchored when the winds pick up.

And the winds always pick up.

SECTION 5: THE SPACE WHERE CUSTODIANS LIVE

Leadership doesn't live on the extremes.
But it doesn't always live dead center either.

It moves along a spectrum, between too little and too much, between silence and noise, between rigidity and drift.

Custodians stay alert.
They adjust with clarity not ego.
Because they understand something most people miss:

Every real virtue lives in tension.
Too little, and it's weakness.
Too much, and it becomes distortion.
There is no perfect middle, only constant calibration.

Courage lives between avoidance and recklessness.

If a child strikes an adult, real courage might look like the adult's restraint, holding back when ego wants to react. In that moment, courage leans closer to avoidance, because control prevents escalation.

But if someone sees a group of people harming someone defenseless, courage might mean stepping in, even if it puts you at risk. In that case, it leans closer to recklessness.

Clarity lives between ambiguity and bluntness.

Clarity doesn't always mean saying everything.
Sometimes it means knowing what the moment can carry and saying only that.

When someone on your team asks, "Is the company okay?" and you don't have the full picture yet, clarity might need to lean toward ambiguity.

You might say, "We're watching it closely, and we'll be straight with you as soon as we know more. You won't be left guessing."

That's not evasion. That's clarity filtered through calm.

But if you've got a colleague who's been drifting, showing up late, missing deadlines, pulling the team down, then clarity has to lean toward bluntness.

You might say, "This has gone on long enough. If something doesn't shift now, you won't be here."

It's not about punishment. It's about alignment.

Clarity bends, but it never blurs.
It delivers what's needed. No more, no less.

Conviction lives between hesitation and stubbornness.

Conviction is a decision. It's not about emotion, it's about alignment. About moving with the Standard you said you would carry, especially when it costs you.

But conviction doesn't always come across the same way.
In some moments, it leans toward hesitation. In others, toward stubbornness.

If someone you trust brings new evidence; something that challenges your position and you stop to weigh it carefully before responding, conviction might look like hesitation.
You're not weak. You're respecting the weight of the moment.

But if you're watching a principle, get stripped down in front of you or your culture eroding, your people being undermined then conviction may need to harden.

You don't stall. You don't soften. You say, "No. This isn't happening on my watch." In that moment, conviction leans toward stubbornness not for pride, but for protection.

Custodians don't confuse indecision with open-mindedness.
And they don't confuse dominance with strength.
They move with conviction, sometimes quiet, sometimes firm.

Always anchored.

Compassion lives between neglect and enabling.

Compassion isn't always gentle, and it isn't always visible. It's not about making people feel better, it's about being useful to them, in the right way, at the right time.

If you have a friend who's ashamed to face you because of something they've done, real compassion might mean staying quiet. You don't chase them. You don't confront them. You give them space and let them come to you. In that moment, compassion leans toward neglect, not out of apathy, but out of respect for their dignity.

But if you have an employee going through a heavy season. missing details, falling short, trying but unraveling, compassion might mean leaning toward enablement. You cover for them. You carry what they can't. You create room they don't know how to ask for. Because people are like trees. They have seasons, too.

Custodians understand that compassion isn't only about consistency. It's about discernment; the ability to read the moment and choose what helps, not just what feels good or looks right. Sometimes compassion shows up. Sometimes it steps back. But it always considers the weight someone is already carrying.

Discipline lives between drift and rigidity.

Discipline isn't about staying tight all the time. It's about knowing when to hold the line and when to give space for learning, struggle, or growth.

If a new employee makes a mistake in their first week, real discipline might look like patience. You don't jump in, micromanage, or correct every detail. You let them feel it, learn from it. In that moment, discipline leans toward drift not because the Standard disappeared, but because timing matters more than control.

But when a clear line has been crossed, when trust is broken, safety is risked, or culture is compromised, discipline has to tighten. It becomes action. Maybe a correction, maybe a separation, but it happens without hesitation. In that case, discipline leans toward rigidity not out of ego, but because clarity must be restored.

Custodians know the difference. They don't confuse patience with passivity, and they don't confuse control with consistency. They lead with discipline not for appearances, but for alignment.

Humility lives between self-doubt and self-importance.

Humility isn't about disappearing. And it's not about being the loudest voice in the room.

It lives between two forms of distortion: self-doubt and self-importance.

If you're stepping into a space where others need room to grow, true humility might lean toward self-doubt.
You second-guess your instinct to speak not because you don't have something to say, but because silence might serve the moment better. It's restraint that looks like uncertainty but it's not.

But if the mission is drifting, and the team is unsure who will lead, humility might need to lean toward self-importance.
You say, "Follow me."
You take the mic. You take the hit. You take the weight.

Not because you're the most important person but because you're the one willing to stand still when everyone else is hesitating.
Humility doesn't vanish.
It doesn't shout.
It reads the moment and moves without ego.

Accountability lives between deflection and self-blame.

Accountability isn't about giving every answer or taking every hit.
It's about knowing what's yours to carry, what needs to be guarded, and what the moment requires.

If you lead a team or hold confidential information and someone confronts you with loaded questions, real accountability might lean toward deflection.

You don't lie. But you also don't expose people who trusted you to carry the weight with discretion.
You keep it tight. You say less. Not because you're hiding but because you've been entrusted.

But if a major failure happens in your department one that affects the mission, breaks trust, or puts others at risk then true accountability will move toward self-blame first.
You step forward and say, "This happened on my watch. I didn't stop it. If consequences follow, the buck starts with me."
That doesn't mean you caused it. But leadership means stepping into responsibility first.

Custodians know the difference.
And they recalibrate based on the situation without dodging what's theirs to carry

Integrity lives between appeasement and self-righteousness.

Integrity isn't about being neutral. It's about being aligned.
And alignment doesn't always look balanced. Sometimes it looks like you're bending. Sometimes it looks like you're standing too hard. But it's always rooted in the same thing: doing what's right based on what's real.

There are moments when integrity leans toward appeasement.

Like when you start to sense someone is exploiting you or your team but you don't have the full picture yet.

You hold back. You observe. You wait.
You don't strike first. Not because you're afraid, but because integrity demands clarity before correction.

You don't confront on a hunch. You wait for proof. So when you move, it holds.

And there are moments when integrity leans toward self-righteousness.

Like when a line gets crossed and you say, "I don't care how normal this is. I'm not doing it."
Even if it makes you look extreme. Even if people roll their eyes.

You draw the line because that's where it belongs even if you're the only one holding it.

Custodians don't confuse silence with weakness or conviction with ego.
They move with integrity not to appear principled, but to live aligned.

SECTION 6: NEVER AT THE PRICE OF...

Custodians adapt. They modernize. They optimize. But they never trade the essential things to get there.

The Oath says what we won't do. This is where it shows up in real decisions:

Custodians do not trade:

- **People for margin** because burnout is never a long-term strategy.
- **Standards for speed** because speed without stability collapses.
- **Trust for convenience** because once trust is gone, it doesn't come back.
- **Safety for savings** because a saved dollar today isn't worth a tragedy tomorrow.
- **Clarity for urgency** because urgent doesn't mean right.
- **Dignity for deliverables** because work should never come at the cost of humanity.

- **Long-term strength for short-term optics** because looking good today means nothing if it breaks tomorrow.
- **Accountability for comfort** because responsibility doesn't get lighter when you ignore it.
- **Respect for results** because no win is worth becoming someone you wouldn't follow.

No win is worth it if it costs what matters most.

Every decision leaves a mark. Some are shallow; forgotten quickly. Others run deep, shaping culture, trust, and futures long after the moment passes. Custodians understand that. That's why they slow things down before they move. They ask the hard questions. They strip away the noise. They don't guess when the stakes are high—they anchor.

Because real leadership isn't about moving faster. It's about moving deliberately. And when the cost shows up—and it always does—Custodians know they paid it for the right reasons. Not for applause. Not for convenience. But for trust.

SECTION 7: WHAT'S SACRED

A lot of people focus on the win. The metric. The scoreboard. The appearance of success. The win isn't what matters. *How* we win is what matters most.

Because, just like everything else in this book, how you win is what builds something real.
And if you build something real, then when your team is truly ready and has the right foundation, you exponentially increase your chance of winning.

Not because you got lucky. Not because things got easier.

But because you're standing on something solid and it holds under pressure.

The win might be delayed. The reward might take time. But the way you get there is what makes it repeatable. Sustainable. Trustworthy. Built to last.

That's why what's sacred matters.

Not everything sacred gets tracked. Not everything sacred gets celebrated.

But these are the things that keep everything else from falling apart:

- A team's endurance because someone protected their time.
- A crew's safety because someone refused to rush.
- A customer's dignity because someone didn't cut corners.
- A system that stayed whole because someone double-checked when no one asked them to.
- A community's trust because someone told the truth when it was easier to stay quiet.
- A colleague's confidence because someone gave credit without needing any.
- A family's rhythm because someone kept showing up even when no one thanked them.

These moments are small. Quiet. Invisible.

But they're sacred.

And when they disappear, everything else starts to break.

Custodians don't guard these things for applause.

They guard them because they know:

If you lose the how, the win doesn't matter.

And if you get the how right, eventually, the win takes care of itself.

SECTION 8: THE PROCESS OVER THE PRIZE

What's sacred isn't protected in the outcome. It's protected in the process.

Custodians focus on the inputs; the work, the care, the discipline behind how things are built, not just what gets built. They understand something shortcuts never teach:

Good input and good process create good outcomes. Anyone can chase a prize. But if the foundation is rushed, hollow, or cracked, the win won't last.

That's why Custodians don't just ask, "Did we win?" They ask harder questions:

- Did we earn it?
- Did we build it the right way?
- Would I sign my name to this in five years?
- Will it still stand when I'm not around to defend it?
- Would I be proud if someone I love found out how this was done?

They refine how they show up. They sharpen how the work gets done. They protect the Standard, even when faster paths are available because they know strong outcomes aren't accidents. Good inputs create strong processes, and strong processes create strong outcomes. They're the byproduct of consistent, disciplined work.

Custodians don't obsess over the scoreboard. They stay anchored in the approach because they understand:

The process is the real prize. Get the process right, and the results will follow.

Maybe not immediately. Maybe not dramatically. But steadily and in ways that endure.

SECTION 9: THE CUSTODIAN COMPASS

Stewardship isn't guesswork. It requires tools. It requires clarity. Especially when the pressure is high.

That's where the Custodian Compass comes in.
Not to hand out easy answers.
Not to guarantee perfection.
But to help leaders move with intention when the weight hits.
Because pressure moments aren't clean.
They're messy. Fast. Emotional.
And without a way to reset, even the best can drift.
The Custodian Compass is built for those moments.

Start With These Six Compass Questions

1. Am I making this choice, or just going along with it?
2. Do I want to make this choice, or am I avoiding the discomfort of pushback?
3. Am I clear, or clouded by fear, ego, pressure, or fatigue?
4. Will this still be the right decision tomorrow, next month, and five years from now?
5. If someone I care about made this same decision, would I back it without hesitation or ask them to rethink it?
6. Would I be proud to explain this to someone I love without changing the story?

If the answers hold up, move forward.
If they're cloudy, pause.

Then Enter the Virtue Flows

These eight flows help return you to the line. Each is tied to a core Custodian virtue. Each exposes a specific kind of drift.

Courage

Speak or stay silent?

Am I staying silent to protect the truth or to protect myself?

Would silence allow harm to go unchecked?

If someone I care about was hurt by my silence, would I regret it?

Lesson: Silence is not always wrong. But it is never neutral.

Conviction

Do I actually believe in this?

Am I deciding based on alignment or fear?

Is this a one-time exception, or am I building a habit?

Would I still make this call if no one noticed?

Lesson: Conviction is not volume. It is the refusal to hide.

Clarity

What's clouding me?

Can I name the emotion pulling me right now?

If I paused for 24 hours, would I still make this choice?

Is the urgency mine, or is it someone else's panic?

Lesson: Speed blurs. Slowing down clarifies.

Discipline

Will this still be right next week?

Is this solving a real problem, or just buying me relief?

Would this hold up without urgency or reward?

If this behavior became the norm, what culture would it create?

Lesson: Do not trade long-term trust for short-term motion.

Accountability

Would I back this if someone else did it?

If my team did this, would I call it leadership?

Would I want someone younger learning from this?

Would I need to explain this decision, or could I pass it on clean?
Lesson: Carry the weight. Without edits.

Integrity

Would I be proud to own this?
Would I still feel clean if my name wasn't attached?
Would someone I admire respect this move as it is?
Am I already planning to reframe this later to make it sound better?
Lesson: If you would hide it, don't do it.

Compassion

Does this decision honor others?
Am I seeing people, or just problems?
Would I want to be on the receiving end of this choice?
Is this leaving someone behind just to get ahead?
Lesson: Compassion is not weakness. It is the refusal to win by devaluing others.

Humility

Am I still a student?
Have I invited honest feedback, or just approval?
Is my ego driving this, or the mission?
Would I still make this call if no one knew it was mine?
Lesson: The mission is bigger than me. Humility keeps it that way.

The Custodian Compass is not a rulebook.

It is a recalibration tool.
It is how stewards return to the line.
Not by luck. Not by habit.

By decision.

SECTION 10: THE FINAL CHARGE

You won't be celebrated for this.
You won't always be understood.
And most of the time, you'll lead when no one's watching.

But someone must hold the line.
Someone must lead when it costs more than it pays.
Someone must carry the weight.

That's what this is.
Not a framework.
Not a style.
A way of life; chosen, built, and carried.

What comes next isn't theory.
It's the vow.

———○———

The following Custodian Creed embodies the essence of the Standard, a timeless commitment to guide through pressure and uncertainty. In the chapters ahead, these principles will transform into actionable commitments, built choice by choice. Let's move forward.

CUSTODIAN CREED

I do not exist to be seen.
I exist to protect what matters.
I move not for applause, but for duty.
I build what will outlive me,
even if no one remembers my name.

I trust the mission more than I trust my fears.
I choose the discipline of action over the comfort of excuses.
I understand that shortcuts only delay the debt
that must one day be paid.

I do not measure my worth by recognition.
I measure it by the quiet, lasting positive impact
on the lives I touch.

I accept that I may never see the harvest.
I accept that my work may be forgotten.
I accept that the world may still fall after I am gone.

But while I am here
I will fight.
I will build.
I will serve.
I will protect.

Because the work itself is the reward.
Because stewardship is the only true inheritance.

There is no way around.
There is no way back.
There is only the way through.

I am a Custodian.
And I endure.

CHAPTER THREE

—— O ——

The Core Commitments

CHOOSING THE CUSTODIAN MINDSET IS A START. LIVING IT TAKES SOMETHING MORE.

In Chapter 2, you decided what kind of leader you want to become: A Custodian who carries the Standard, protects what matters, and refuses shortcuts. But a mindset alone won't hold under pressure. You need clear, practical commitments you can lean on, habits tested by reality, sharpened by experience, and flexible enough to work in real life.

That's exactly what you'll find in this chapter.

The **five commitments** ahead aren't rigid rules carved in stone. They're battle-tested practices designed to anchor your decisions, shape your responses, and steady your leadership when it matters most. Think of them as your compass when clarity fades and as guardrails when temptation calls.

Because believing in a Standard doesn't change anything. Living by these commitments does.

1. People First, Always

People aren't part of the work. They are the work.

Not the logo, the spreadsheets, or the systems.
Not the building, the platform, or the brand.

Putting people first isn't just the right thing. **It's the only thing**.

- It's the teacher staying late to help one more student.
- The nurse covering an extra shift because someone needs care.
- The parent quietly holding their family steady, day after day.
- The small business owner keeping the lights on, even when margins are thin.
- The developer fixing code at midnight because someone depends on it.
- The frontline worker who shows up, even without thanks.

If these people don't show up, everything stops.

Putting people first means a focus on:

Human-Centered Design. Design teams, schedules, and systems around actual human beings with real limits, real needs, and real lives, not around idealized versions on paper.

Proactive Support. Anticipate needs before they become emergencies, to create stability instead of a scramble for solutions.

Shared Stewardship. Protect people's trust, time, and health as if they were your own.

Gratitude in Action. Express gratitude through meaningful actions, not empty gestures.

Relationship-First Thinking. Prioritize long-term relationships over short-term convenience or efficiency.

Hard choices still happen. People still disappoint.
But the answer isn't to squeeze the best until they break.

It's to create environments, at home, at school, at work that refuse to treat people as disposable.

Because when people understand they genuinely matter, something shifts.

> *They don't just produce. They invest.*
> *They don't just follow the mission, they carry it.*

That's how trust deepens.

How culture strengthens.

How families, classrooms, companies, and communities become unshakeable.

People are always the long game.

I can't count how many times in my life I was driven by this commitment.
I don't want to list them. I don't want to talk about them.
This isn't a badge or a résumé point. It's personal.

Because when you really put someone first, when you show up in a way that matters, it's between you and them.

- They know the truth. And that's enough.
- No one needs to brag. No one needs to know.

But if this chapter helps someone make that kind of decision without hesitation, without needing permission, then it's worth it. Because putting people first doesn't need an audience. It just needs to be real.

And yes it gets criticized.

It's not always considered a "smart" decision.
On paper, it rarely looks efficient.

But I'm not leading paper. I'm not leading numbers.

I'm leading people—with families, with futures, with real weight on their backs—and I don't take their livelihood lightly.

If I were leading robots, maybe the math would matter more.

But we're building something with humans.

So I'll keep leading like a human no matter what the spreadsheet says.

2. Do It Right

There are two ways to do things:

> *Do things that pass for now.*
> *Do things that last.*

Doing it right isn't about approval, it's about respect for the work itself.

It's about integrity, the kind people feel even when no one's checking.

That integrity begins long before action. It means:

- Not making promises that can't be honored.
- Refusing to hide problems just to get ahead.
- Saying "not yet" when that's the truthful answer.
- Not passing issues downstream for someone else to fix.

Once the action starts, integrity shows up in how we work:

- Communicating clearly, without assumptions.
- Executing carefully, not hastily.
- Asking questions proactively.
- Catching mistakes before they spread.

And when problems inevitably arise, the response is clear and consistent:

- Face the issue directly.
- Don't conceal, don't deflect, don't stall.
- Own it openly and repair it thoroughly.

Because doing it right isn't merely about quality—it's about character:

- No shortcuts simply because no one's watching.
- No inflated numbers or empty promises.
- No settling for "technically correct."

Whether it's building a house, writing code, teaching a class, or running a business, if it carries a person's name, it should hold up.

Not just today. For years.

Doing it right means the work endures. Trust strengthens. And future teams build upon foundations rather than repairing damage.

It means pride remains intact, clients return by choice, and communities benefit over the long run.

It's never about perfection. It's always about integrity.

When a person's name or word is attached—
Make sure it means something.

3. Spend Tight, Invest Right

Anyone can spend money. Anyone can slash costs.
The discipline lies in knowing exactly when to do each.

Spending tight isn't about starving resources, it's about cutting waste.

Investing right isn't about lavish spending, it's about fueling strength.

Whether it's a household budget, a small business, a school, or a nonprofit, the principle stays consistent:
Spend intentionally.
Invest strategically.

Spending tight means:

- Ensuring every dollar has a clear purpose.
- Eliminating activities, tools, or traditions that drain resources without delivering value.
- Letting go of habits justified only by tradition or convenience.

But tight spending alone isn't enough. Without strategic investment, budgets starve the very future they should be protecting.

Investing right means deliberately and thoughtfully allocating resources for:

- Tools and technology that simplify tasks and enhance effectiveness.
- Processes and systems that eliminate friction rather than create it.
- People who generate lasting value, not just immediate output.
- Training and education that empower people, rather than merely completing box-checking exercises.

A business that underpays will lose talent, no matter how lean the balance sheet looks.

A school that cuts the training and development budget for teacher training weakens classrooms, no matter how budget-friendly it seems.

The art is in balance:

- Frugal, but not short-sighted.
- Disciplined, but not rigid.
- Efficient, without losing sight of purpose.

Spending tight keeps resources sharp.
Investing right ensures those resources create something lasting.

Financial discipline isn't about doing less—it's about doing better.

4. Dream So Big

True impact is measured not by what individuals accomplish alone, but by what continues long after their work is done.

To dream big means to imagine ambitions so expansive that they cannot be achieved within a single lifetime. It means intentionally making decisions through the perspective of generations yet to come, decisions that may not pay off immediately but create lasting foundations for the future.

Dreaming big requires:

Building foundations strong enough to endure beyond one generation.

Planting seeds that others will nurture and harvest.

Passing down wisdom and vision generously, without hesitation or insecurity.

Addressing problems at their roots, rather than choosing short-term fixes.

Choosing paths whose true significance and benefit might only become clear decades later.

True vision is never limited to one person's timeline or capabilities. If a vision collapses once the original visionary departs, it wasn't genuinely a vision, it was merely possession.

The strongest legacies are those whose significance expands and whose value deepens with every new generation that embraces them.

The boldest dreams are always bigger than any single dreamer.

5. Never Lose Your Uniqueness

Every person, every family, every team, every organization has a distinct identity, *not just a brand, a slogan, or a statement.* An essence built from consistent choices, behaviors, and values.

Identity isn't found in mission statements.
It reveals itself through actions under pressure.

It's in what's rewarded, what's tolerated, and what's swiftly corrected.

Every environment takes on the character of the people shaping it.

- When someone leads with clarity, those around them become sharper.
- When ego dominates, politics thrive.
- Shortcuts teach others that standards are negotiable.
- But genuine humility, consistency, and authenticity inspire the same in return.

Protecting uniqueness means actively preserving these core values. It means:

Saying no to opportunities, people, or projects that dilute core values.

Upholding standards instead of fitting into convenient molds.

Staying consistent, regardless of circumstance.

Remembering what creates strength and not sacrificing it for temporary comfort.

Above all, it means:

- Refusing to simply perform.
- Refusing to compromise personal truth for external approval.

Because the moment you trade your uniqueness, what's left isn't you, it's a version built to please.

When integrity becomes a mask, identity starts slipping away quietly and subtly.

It starts small: a convenient compromise, a silent agreement, delayed confrontation. These moments feel strategic, even mature.

But eventually, something changes.
The essence fades. Integrity weakens.
A voice grows silent.
Until one day, a person no longer recognizes who they've become.

I've felt that erosion before—the kind that doesn't announce itself but shows up quietly in how you compromise, delay, or stay silent, just to blend in. Uniqueness doesn't disappear all at once; you give it away, one small concession at a time.

But the world doesn't need another copy.

It needs original voices, original perspectives—people who stand anchored in conviction.

Protecting uniqueness isn't about refusing growth.

It's about ensuring growth comes authentically—from honest reflection, courageous correction, and internal clarity.

Being uncomfortable, evolving, and learning are all essential. *But never at the cost of personal authenticity.*

Integrity demands being true to oneself, even when pressured to conform.

Stay uncomfortable if that's what it takes.

But never lose your uniqueness.

These five commitments aren't about perfection, they're about direction.

Each one is designed to move principles from intention to action, from belief to daily behavior. Together, they form a framework sturdy enough to withstand pressure, temptation, and uncertainty. By putting people first, doing it right, spending tight and investing right, dreaming so big that future generations carry the vision, and never losing uniqueness, individuals can create something truly enduring.

These commitments don't guarantee easy paths or quick victories. They guarantee clarity under pressure and integrity in every choice.

Carry these commitments and the Custodian Standard moves from a philosophy you admire to the life you lead.

CHAPTER FOUR

The Standard in Motion

CARRYING IT DAILY IS THE REAL TEST.

Commitments look great written down, but unless they are lived, they don't mean a thing.

- Chapter 3 set the bar.
- Chapter 4 is about meeting it. Every single day.

This isn't about philosophy or grand speeches. It's about habits—simple and clear that you can apply daily.

This chapter strips away excuses, complexity, and ambiguity.

The real work doesn't live in the big moments; it lives in small, daily choices. Leaders don't wait for drama to show their strength. They show it quietly, consistently, in every action they take.

Here's exactly how to move every day, not just when it's easy but especially when it's not.

SECTION 1: TACTICAL BEHAVIORS

The TACTIC shows you how to move when it counts. It consists of six behaviors: **T**one-setting, **A**cting with Purpose, **C**hecking for

Alignment, **T**alking with Precision, **I**dentifying Emotions, and Closing the Loop through **R**esponding with Clarity.

1. Tone First (T)

Every interaction, every conversation, every classroom, every family discussion, every work meeting they have an unspoken tone.

Either it's intentionally set, or it's left up for grabs.

Most people hesitate to set the tone first, hoping things will naturally fall into place. But hoping rarely works. Instead, uncertainty, confusion, or frustration fills the silence.

Setting the tone early means choosing clarity proactively:

- **At Home:** Before difficult family conversations, clearly state, "We're here to solve this, not to argue. Let's stay calm and honest." One clear statement immediately sets a cooperative tone.
- **In the Classroom:** At the beginning of class, clarify expectations explicitly: "Today we're focusing on this lesson. Let's keep our questions related so everyone stays on track." Now students know exactly how to engage.
- **At Work:** Start meetings explicitly: "The goal here is to make a decision, not to debate endlessly. Let's listen carefully and stay sharp." Immediately people know exactly how to contribute productively.
- **One-on-One:** Before a tough conversation, set clarity first: "This talk might be uncomfortable, but I want honesty above everything." Now trust is built from the start.

Whoever speaks first sets the energy clearly.

Don't let uncertainty, confusion, or someone else's mood define the room. Take control early, clearly, intentionally every time.

2. Act with Purpose (A)

Purpose isn't about chasing outcomes; it's about clarity behind every action you take.

It's the simple habit of knowing exactly why you're doing something, instead of just doing it because it's next on the list.

Here's how purpose works in real, daily situations:

- **Before speaking:** Quickly pause and ask yourself: "Am I speaking to be understood, or just to fill silence?" Immediately, your communication becomes clearer.
- **In difficult conversations:** Clarify your intent upfront: "Am I here to listen and understand, or am I here to defend?" This instantly sets your tone and approach clearly.
- **During routine tasks:** Remind yourself quickly, "I'm doing this because it's necessary or helpful and not just because it's automatic." Your tasks become meaningful, even when they're mundane.
- **When responding to requests:** Pause briefly to identify why you're saying yes or no. "Am I responding out of obligation, habit, or genuine intent?" Your decisions immediately become clearer and more intentional.

Purpose doesn't mean chasing some future result, it means ensuring there is clarity behind every action you take.

It's a small habit that changes how you move through your day, with precision and intention, every single time.

3. Check for Alignment (C)

Assumptions are expensive. They cost time, energy, and trust.

Most teams don't fall apart because people stop caring, they drift because they thought they were aligned but weren't. They walked away from a meeting with different understandings, different expectations, and no confirmation of clarity.

That drift is preventable. And leaders who care about their team's time and trust don't hope for alignment they confirm it.

Here's exactly how to build the habit:

After giving instructions: Don't ask, "Got it?" Instead, ask, "Can you walk me through what you heard?" This reveals gaps before they grow.

At the end of a meeting: Always ask, "Who's doing what by when?" Don't let people guess what the next move is.

When receiving direction: Reflect back what you heard. Say, "Just to confirm, you want me to do X by Y. Correct?" It shows professionalism and it protects your time.

Clarity isn't extra. It's essential. And checking for alignment isn't micromanagement it's leadership.

Because when alignment is assumed, mistakes multiply.
But when it's confirmed, momentum builds.

Alignment doesn't slow the team down. It speeds them up, because no one's carrying the extra weight of confusion.

4. Talk with Precision (T)

Most people talk too much especially under pressure.

They fill the silence because silence feels awkward. They explain, then re-explain, hoping clarity eventually emerges.

Precision isn't about sounding professional or polished. It's about making sure what needs to be understood is.

Whether someone is:

- Resolving a disagreement
- Teaching a child
- Presenting to a group, or
- Simply giving instructions

Precision always matters.

Here's exactly how to practice precision:

Say Less, Mean More: Before speaking, pause for two seconds. Quickly clarify exactly what needs to be understood, then say only that.

One Idea at a Time: Instead of lumping several thoughts together, clearly separate each idea. Finish one point fully before moving to the next.

Check for Understanding: After delivering important information, pause again. Ask explicitly, "Does this make sense?" or "Are we aligned?" Don't guess.

Precision creates clarity. Clarity solves problems faster, reduces conflict, and builds trust, no matter who's speaking or listening.

5. Identify Emotions, Respond with Clarity: (I)

Respond Clearly, Not Emotionally.

Under pressure, most people react first, then think later.

Someone gets defensive, someone else shuts down, and suddenly clarity disappears.

Emotional reactions rarely solve anything they only escalate confusion, tension, or mistakes.

Responding clearly isn't about denying emotions. It's about pausing long enough to separate immediate feelings from necessary actions.

Here's how this works practically:

Pause First: *The next time a conversation turns tense or a situation feels charged, pause for two full breaths before speaking. It sounds small, but this pause is the difference between reacting and responding.*

Name the Feeling Clearly (without Blaming): *Instead of snapping back defensively, clarify calmly: "This feels tense," or "I'm sensing frustration." Naming a feeling creates clarity without judgment or blame.*

Restate the Problem in Simple Terms: *After acknowledging the emotion, immediately restate the issue clearly: "So, the real issue we need to solve right now is…"*

Focus on the Next Clear Step: *Instead of dwelling on who's right or wrong, clearly ask, "What's the best next step?" or "How do we move forward from here?"*

This behavior works everywhere:

- In a disagreement at home, choose calm clarity over emotional escalation.
- When criticized at work, clearly restate the issue rather than defending immediately.
- If a conversation becomes heated then use a simple, clear statement rather than matching emotional intensity.

Emotions are normal but letting them control the response isn't.

Clarity comes from choosing to respond deliberately and precisely, every single time.

6. Close Every Loop (C)

Open loops drain energy, trust, and momentum. They clutter the mind and slow people down. Every unfinished task or incomplete conversation quietly steals attention from what matters.

Closing loops isn't complicated. It means finishing what gets started, completely, reliably, every single time.

Here's exactly how it works in practice:

Conversations: Before leaving, a simple check: "Anything left unresolved?" If there is, handle it immediately not later, not maybe.

Promises: Don't promise casually. Once promised, deliver. When done, confirm directly: "It's finished." People don't guess; they know.

Small Tasks: If something can be completed quickly, finish it on the spot. No delays, no extra noise.

End-of-Day Checks: At day's end, do a quick review for unfinished business. Anything left open gets resolved or clearly scheduled, right then not tomorrow.

This isn't perfection. It's discipline. If it gets opened, it gets closed. Every loop, every time.

TACTIC is not theory. It's practical. It's how you:

- Eliminate confusion
- Prevent drift, and
- Keep your team and your decisions tight.

These six behaviors aren't optional; they're how standards hold under pressure.

If you're serious about carrying weight, this is your daily system. No guessing. No drama. Just clarity, action, and follow-through.

SECTION 2: DISCIPLINED—*SHARP*—HABITS

SHARP habits are what separate people who flash once from those who last: **S**how Up Prepared. **H**old the Line in Private. **A**ct Daily, Not in Bursts. **R**esharpen the Blade. **P**rove the Standard by Modeling.

These keep you honed for awareness and smart execution every day.

> *Tactical behaviors help people act decisively in the moment. But consistent execution doesn't come from moments—it comes from habits.*

Disciplined habits aren't flashy:

- They're quietly powerful routines built intentionally, practiced daily, and internalized deeply.
- They shape decisions long before pressure hits, turning clear thinking from something people do occasionally into something they do automatically.

These habits don't rely on motivation they rely on discipline. They aren't complicated, but they demand consistency. They're the quiet actions practiced so regularly they become reflexes, the invisible patterns that define someone clearly when things get noisy or chaotic.

Here's exactly how to build and practice them every day:

1. Show up Prepared (S)

Most people wait until the last minute. They assume they'll rise to the occasion, but people don't rise under pressure, they sink to the level of their preparation.

Preparing before it counts isn't complicated. It's the discipline of thinking ahead and getting ready before being forced to act.

Practically, it looks like this:

The night before: Take five minutes and preview tomorrow—what matters most, what's expected, and what might go wrong. No drama, just practical foresight.

Before difficult conversations: Don't wing it. Write down key points or responses beforehand. Know clearly what needs to be said, so pressure doesn't twist words into regrets.

When facing decisions: Imagine scenarios ahead of time—not obsessively, just practically. People who consider problems before they happen make smarter choices when they do.

Before presentations, meetings, or tasks: Review the agenda or purpose quickly beforehand. Be clear on objectives ahead of time, instead of figuring it out midstream.

Disciplined preparation doesn't require hours, just a few clear moments ahead of time. It's a small habit, repeated daily, that quietly builds readiness, confidence, and results.

2. Hold Standards without Witnesses (H)

Most people hold standards when someone's watching but character isn't defined by public performance. It's defined by quiet discipline when nobody sees.

Holding standards without witnesses means doing what's right consistently, even when it's inconvenient, unnoticed, or unrewarded.

Practically, this looks simple:

Small tasks: Finishing with care, even when nobody checks. Quality doesn't depend on who's looking.

Promises: Keeping commitments without reminders or follow-ups. Reliable people don't wait for oversight; they act because they gave their word.

Personal discipline: Doing the right thing privately, not because someone demands it but simply because it's right.

Integrity in small things: Cleaning up messes nobody saw, taking responsibility before its noticed, fixing mistakes unnoticed. Integrity isn't loud; it's subtle and silent.

Holding standards without witnesses isn't about proving character, *it's simply having character.*

It's a disciplined habit practiced daily, quietly defining exactly who a person is, even when nobody's watching.

3. Act Daily, not in Bursts (A)

Most people try to fix problems with intensity.

They cram.
They sprint.
They push hard, briefly.
Then they burn out.

Consistency beats intensity every single time. It's not flashy, but it works.
Consistency means showing up steadily—even if progress seems slow. It's about habitually choosing small actions repeatedly, rather than huge efforts occasionally.

Practically, it looks like this:
Learn a skill: Practicing deliberately for fifteen minutes every day not for three exhausting hours once a week.

Get healthier: Eating slightly better every meal not obsessing over one perfect diet day.

Relationships: Checking in briefly but regularly, instead of one huge conversation after problems pile up.

Work or study: Spending a clear, dedicated hour each day, instead of pulling all-nighters under pressure.

People who rely on intensity burn bright, then fade quickly. Those who choose consistency quietly outlast them every time.

It's not complicated.

It's steady discipline, practiced daily.

4. Resharpen the Blade Daily (R)

Skills don't stay sharp by accident. They dull quietly over time if they're not actively maintained.

Sharpening the blade daily isn't dramatic, it's disciplined and steady practice.

It means regularly improving a little, deliberately staying fresh, and always refining.

Here's exactly how this works in practice:

Daily learning: Taking fifteen deliberate minutes to read, practice, or learn something specific—not hours occasionally, but small intentional daily efforts.

Immediate feedback: Asking someone directly, "What's one thing that could have been done better?" immediately after finishing a task. Improvement happens clearly and quickly.

Conscious self-checks: Quickly reviewing recent performance each day, not obsessively but practically. A simple question: "What one small thing can improve tomorrow?"

Routine drills: Practicing basic skills regularly, even if already proficient. Professionals don't stop practicing just because they're good, they practice to stay good.

Sharpening the blade daily isn't perfectionism; it's practical discipline.

People who quietly sharpen their skills each day outperform those who rely on occasional bursts of effort, every single time.

5. Prove the Standard by Modeling (P)

People don't follow words, they follow actions.

> *Standards don't spread through speeches or policies;*
> *they spread through daily behaviors people see and copy.*

Modeling the Standard relentlessly means consistently living what others should follow. No exceptions, no excuses, no days off.

In practice, it looks straightforward:

Showing, not just telling: If punctuality matters, be consistently on time. If respect matters, treat everyone respectfully, every interaction. People notice what's real—not what's said.

Owning mistakes openly: When something goes wrong, own it immediately and without excuses. Leaders who model accountability quietly teach everyone else to do the same.

Staying consistent under pressure: Behaving the same way on bad days as on good ones—not changing standards just because it's tough. People trust consistency, not perfection.

Doing small things right: Cleaning up, staying organized, being polite. Standards start small. Practiced and modeled consistently, they become the norm.

Relentlessly modeling the Standard isn't flashy, it's quietly powerful.

> *People don't do what's expected; they do what's demonstrated.*
> *Show it every day, and the Standard spreads itself.*

The five SHARP habits:

- Protect your edge
- Help you stay durable.

They don't rely on motivation—they rely on discipline.

Practiced consistently, they become your reflexes when pressure hits.

Stay sharp. No excuses.

Discipline is the daily practice that keeps sharpness real.

Sharpness fades without discipline, just as strength fades without training.

CHAPTER FIVE

Protect the Work

PROTECTION IS KEY

The previous chapters laid the foundation:

Clear commitments.
Disciplined habits.
Practical behaviors stacked with consistency.

But building by itself isn't enough.

Everything people build quietly breaks down if left unattended:

- Standards
- Resources
- Trust
- Culture

The objective of this chapter is simple:

Show exactly how to safeguard and maintain what's already been built.

Because protecting the work isn't passive. It's not something you do only when there's time.

It's deliberate. It's daily. And if you stop tending to it, you lose it.

Below, I'll give clear methods to guard critical resources, defend standards before they slip, and protect the integrity of the culture.

It's not about slogans. It's about making sure effort doesn't get wasted and progress doesn't get lost.

Building something worthwhile is hard enough.

Sustaining it takes just as much discipline and even more vigilance.

SECTION 1: PROTECT WHAT'S IN MOTION

The first step is to protect what is already alive, what's moving, working, carrying weight today.

Because drift doesn't announce itself. It begins quietly, in small compromises and unchecked habits.

What is not protected deteriorates, one layer at a time.

There are four critical lines of defense:

> *The effort.*
> *The asset.*
> *The Standard.*
> *The edge.*

Protect the Effort

Effort is expensive.

It requires time, energy, focus, discipline, and people.

The worst failure isn't losing because of a bad idea.

> *It's wasting strength on work that didn't have a real chance of success.*

Without discipline at the front end, even the strongest teams, families, companies, and missions exhaust themselves. Not from lack of skill, but from chasing work that was flawed from the start.

Protecting the effort means slowing down long enough to ask the right questions:

- Where are we actually trying to go?
- What will real success require, not just today, but over time?
- Are people being positioned to succeed, or are they being set up to burn out?
- Are we fighting real battles or just scrambling because no one thought ahead?

Good intentions don't protect strength.

Good preparation does.

A solid path won't guarantee an easy road.

But it gives the work somewhere to land and keeps momentum from leaking out before it even builds.

This discipline shows up everywhere:

- A teacher who structures lessons, so students peak at the right time.
- A nurse who organizes a shift, so chaos doesn't swallow patient care.
- A builder who sequences a project, so the field stays ahead of the deadline, not behind it.
- A parent who sets anchors at the start of the day, so small fires don't eat up all the time.
- A business owner who designs work that nourishes people and doesn't just extract from them.

Protecting the effort isn't about being perfect.
It's about refusing to waste what matters most: **people's strength, attention, and energy.**

Because once the work starts, the real cost begins.
And if the foundation wasn't strong enough, everyone pays, whether they saw it coming or not.

> *Planning isn't paperwork.*
> *It's leadership in motion.*

Start clean. Set the right path.

Protect the effort because *strength isn't free.*

Protect the Asset

Every system has a critical asset.

It's not always the loudest part.
It's not always the most obvious.

But it's the one thing that, if lost, breaks everything else around it.

- On a **construction crew**, it might be the field team's strength and focus.
- In a **hospital**, it's the nurses' presence of mind when minutes matter.
- In a **household**, it's the emotional steadiness that holds the family together.
- In a **small business**, it's the trust and resilience that keep operations from falling apart when pressure hits.

Protecting the asset starts with identifying it.

That means looking past titles, appearances, and numbers and asking:

- What part of this system cannot be replaced easily?

- What strength, if weakened, would slow or stop everything else?
- Where would failure cause a ripple that doesn't stop?

Once the critical asset is clear, protection becomes the real work:

Don't burn it out. Running harder isn't a strategy if it leaves no one standing.

Don't bury it under noise. Systems fail when the essentials get lost under distractions.

Don't stretch it just to chase numbers. Margins mean nothing if the foundation cracks.

Protecting the asset also means creating stability. Not comfort, not ease but *stability*.

Stability doesn't mean the absence of pressure. It means pressure is applied in ways that strengthen, not fracture.

Children need it to grow.
Teams need it to execute proficiently.
Missions need it to overcome disruption.
Communities need it to rebuild when storms hit.

Stability doesn't happen by accident. It has to be built into the environment through:

- **Systems** that hold when plans fail.
- **Expectations** that stay firm when conditions shift.
- **Standards** that don't buckle when shortcuts appear.

Protecting the asset also means protecting the culture around it, and showing no tolerance for:

Shortcuts disguised as "speed."
Disrespect especially toward those doing the real work.
Burnout celebrated as "commitment."

Because when the asset gets compromised, everything else, morale, performance, trust they start to evaporate quietly.

Leaders who understand this don't waste energy fixing symptoms.

They defend the core every day, even when no one's applauding it.

Identify the asset.
Support it.
Stabilize it.
Protect it.

Protect the asset because *once it breaks, everything else follows.*

Protect the Standard

Standards don't get tested when everything is running smooth. They get tested when something breaks.

Mistakes will happen.
Conditions will change.
People will miss things.
Pressure will hit harder than expected.

The test isn't whether problems show up.

The test is how the Standard holds or doesn't when they do.

Protecting the Standard doesn't mean pretending mistakes won't happen.

It means dealing with them quickly, cleanly, and without excuses.

When a mistake surfaces:

Call it out. Early, directly, without drama.

Own it fully. No dodging. No spinning it to look better.

Fix it properly. Not patches. Not delays. Repair it so it doesn't repeat.

Strengthen what cracked. Make the system better than it was before.

The goal isn't blame.
The goal is protection.

Because every unaddressed mistake leaves a mark.
Every delayed response weakens the culture around the work.

When leaders ignore small breaks, larger ones follow.

Protecting the Standard means refusing to trade long-term strength for short-term comfort.
It means dealing with the uncomfortable moments before they turn into permanent cracks.

This applies everywhere:

- A **coach** who corrects a sloppy practice before it shows up in the game.
- A **nurse** who flags a near-miss before it becomes a tragedy.
- A **foreman** who fixes a small error before it shuts down the site.
- A **parent** who addresses small lies before trust erodes.

Owning the small things protects the bigger things.

Protecting the Standard doesn't require perfection.
It requires conviction, especially when it would be easier to stay quiet, shift blame, or let it slide.

Because when leaders flinch, the Standard bleeds.
And once that bleeding starts, it's hard to stop.

Call it.
Own it.
Fix it.
Protect it.

Protect the Standard, *strength isn't measured when things are easy. It's measured by what gets protected when pressure hits.*

Protect the Edge

The sharpness that builds something worthwhile isn't automatic and it doesn't last without work.

Every strong system, every strong leader, every strong team starts with an edge:

The ability to stay prepared, stay precise, stay real.

But edges don't stay sharp on their own. They dull quietly.

Not from failure but from comfort.
Not from pressure but from believing the work is already finished.

It starts small:

- Skills stop getting refreshed.
- Assumptions replace questions.
- Wins get taken for granted.
- Feedback gets avoided instead of welcomed.

And slowly, almost invisibly the sharpness that built strength starts to erode.

Protecting the edge isn't about staying busy.

It's about staying real.
It means staying coachable when others get defensive.
It means practicing fundamentals when others coast.
It means asking hard questions when others assume they already know.

Protecting the edge shows up everywhere:

- The **craftsman** who still checks measurements after years of experience.

- The **teacher** who still studies new methods after decades in the classroom.
- The **business owner** who still double-checks the basics after building success.
- The **parent** who still learns and adapts as the seasons of life change.

Protecting the edge also means protecting against ego.

Ego is the fastest way to go dull.

The second someone starts believing they're too experienced to double-check, too important to listen, or too established to adjust, they've already started slipping.

The edge isn't about confidence.

It's about discipline.

Stay uncomfortable enough to stay sharp.
Stay humble enough to stay growing.

Because once the edge dulls, the system follows.

Sharpen daily.
Question assumptions.
Stay a student, even after becoming a master.

Protect the edge, *everything built on it depends on it.*

SECTION 2: PROTECT WHAT CARRIES THE WORK FORWARD

Protecting today's work isn't enough.
If it's going to last, it must be carried forward

By people
By culture
By environments that stay steady when pressure rises.

This section focuses on the second half of real protection: defending the spaces and the people that will outlive today's work.

Protect the Room

Pressure shows up without warning.
It doesn't care how prepared people were yesterday.
It doesn't care how strong the system looked last week.
It moves fast. It strips away polish.
And it exposes exactly what was real and what wasn't.

When pressure hits, the room decides what happens next.

Not the plan.
Not the policies.
The room.

- The tone.
- The energy.
- The discipline or the lack of it.

Protecting the room isn't about pretending nothing is wrong.
It's about holding steady long enough for real leadership to move.

When everything tightens:

- Speak less. Move sharper.
- Lower the volume. Shorten the distance.
- Focus on decisions, not distractions.

Strong rooms don't stay calm by accident.
They stay calm because someone protects the environment when everyone else is reacting.

It happens in every field:

- A **teacher** who steadies a classroom when panic hits.
- A **paramedic** who brings order to an accident scene.

- A **project lead** who absorbs pressure so the crew can keep building.
- A **parent** who neutralizes fear before it spreads through a family.

Protecting the room doesn't require having every answer.
It requires presence—real presence that steadies others without empty promises or false confidence.

When crisis hits:

- State what's known. State what's unknown.
- Tell the truth faster than the rumor mill can.
- Buy time if needed but don't let panic set the terms.

And when the immediate storm passes, real leaders don't just move on.

They debrief. They study where the breaks happened, and they reinforce the system before the next hit.

Because leadership isn't just how someone moves during the calm. It's how they shape the environment when calm disappears.

Protect the room *when everything else breaks. People will remember whether the foundation held or collapsed.*

Protect the Circle

Systems don't carry themselves forward.
People do. And not just any people—the right ones.

The ones who lived the Standard when no one was watching.
The ones who carried the weight without needing applause.
The ones who stayed steady when others drifted.

Protecting the circle means protecting the few who earned the right to carry it forward.

It starts early. The circle doesn't build itself through convenience or politics.

It builds through tested weight. Through people who showed, over time, that they could be trusted with something heavier than themselves.

Once that foundation exists, it becomes leadership's job to defend it.

That means:

- **Backing the right people** when mistakes happen, instead of letting noise dictate decisions.
- **Sharpening them** instead of sheltering them—coaching hard because they deserve it, not because they need it.
- **Clearing obstacles** so they can lead without being drowned in distractions.
- **Protecting the Standard** even more fiercely around them because they aren't carrying a slogan, they're carrying proof.

And just as important:

Guard the perimeter of the circle with discipline.

Not everyone earns a place inside.

The wrong additions to the circle: those chasing titles, credit, shortcuts, or status they don't just slow the mission down. They weaken the work that real Custodians fought to protect. If someone won't carry the weight, they don't belong in the circle, no matter their resume, and no matter their connections.

Protect the circle. When a system forgets who made it strong, it doesn't just lose people.

It loses the very proof that it ever worked.

CHAPTER SIX

The Legacy Lens

Everything built so far, the Standard, the discipline, the work worth protecting was never meant to stop here.

It wasn't built just for the next deadline.
Or the next project.
Or the next scoreboard that fits inside a quarter.

It was built to be handed forward and stronger than it started.

Because real leadership isn't just carrying the weight.
It's preparing it for the ones who will carry it next.

The Legacy Lens demands a shift:
from protecting what's working today,
to protecting what will survive tomorrow.

Not fame.
Not applause.
Not personal validation.

IMPACT.

Measured quietly

In the systems that hold.

In the people who stand stronger because of how the work was carried.
In the places where the Standard stays alive, and long after the previous generations are gone.

This chapter isn't about adding more to carry.
It's about seeing the real reason you carry it at all.

Because no matter how strong the work looks today—
if it doesn't survive beyond the hands that built it,
it was never real strength to begin with.

LEGACY ISN'T ABOUT FAME, IT'S ABOUT IMPACT

Most people never shift their lens far enough.

They build for applause. They chase titles. They mistake visibility for value.

But fame isn't legacy. It fades too fast.
Recognition isn't legacy. Attention moves on.
Noise isn't legacy. Applause stops.

Real legacy isn't measured by how many people know your name. It's measured by how many lives stand stronger because of the work you carried.

And most real legacy isn't celebrated while it's happening.

It's lived quietly.
It's protected without cameras.
It's passed forward without needing to be seen.

Legacy shows up in the structure that doesn't collapse when the founder is gone.

- In the Standard that still holds when pressure hits a generation later.

- In the names no one remembers but whose impact runs through everything that still works.

Legacy shows up in:

- A **family** that stays together because someone set the standard early.
- A **team** that holds its edge even after leadership changes.
- A **system** that still protects people long after the architect is forgotten.

Fame is loud.

Legacy is quiet.

Fame is temporary.

Legacy is transferable.

One fades with attention.

The other compounds across generations.

Real builders don't chase the first.

They protect the second.

Because legacy isn't about being seen.
It's about building something that stays.

WHAT REAL LEGACY LOOKS LIKE

Real legacy doesn't announce itself.

It's not carved into plaques.
It's not built on slogans.
It's not carried by noise.
It moves differently.

Real legacy is built through actions that outlive the people who made them. It's carried through systems, standards, and behaviors that stay steady whether or not anyone remembers who first set them.

The patterns are simple:

- **Weight that is carried without needing credit.**
  The work matters more than the attention it receives.

- **Decisions that are made for the next season, not the next spotlight.**
  Short-term wins aren't worth sacrificing long-term strength.

- **Standards that survive distance.**
  The real measure isn't how someone acts under supervision it's how they move when no one's watching.

- **Structures that protect people after the builder steps away.**

  If a system collapses when the founder leaves, it was never strong. It was just loud.

- **Principles passed down, not just tasks.**
  Skills can be taught quickly. Standards take generations.

Real legacy doesn't feel urgent while it's being built.
It feels quiet. Routine. Almost invisible.

It lives in how people talk to each other
when no one else is listening.

It lives in how decisions get made
when nobody's prescribing the outcome.

It lives in the strength that holds under pressure
without needing a rescue.

That's the real proof:
When the pressure hits and the original builder isn't there, the work still holds.

That's when you know the weight was carried right.
Not just for today.
But for tomorrow.

THE COST OF A HOLLOW LEGACY

Not every structure survives its builder.
Not every system deserves to.

When people chase legacy for themselves, when they build for attention, for applause or for control the foundation never holds.

It might look strong for a while.
It might create noise, and gather followers, funding, and momentum.

But hollow work always collapses when the hands holding it let go.

The cost of a hollow legacy isn't just the collapse of the builder's reputation.
It's the damage left behind:

- Teams that fracture because the Standard was never real, it was artificial performance.
- Systems that break because discipline was superficial, not lived.
- Cultures that rot because shortcuts were tolerated as long as results looked good.
- Families, businesses, communities that drift because no one was taught how to carry the weight after the spotlight moved on.

Nothing collapses faster than a system built around ego. Nothing rots faster than a culture built on short-term wins.

The damage isn't visible right away.

It shows up years later, in the people forced to rebuild without knowing what strength looks like anymore.

That's the real cost of hollow work:

The next ones pay the price.

The ones who needed something steady are left cleaning up something broken.
Real leadership doesn't just protect today's mission.
It protects the next generation's footing.

Because the job isn't just to carry weight while it's easy.
It's to hand forward something that doesn't buckle when real storms come.

When legacy is hollow, nothing survives except excuses.

When it's real, strength outlives memory.

REAL LEGACY EXAMPLES

Real legacy isn't made in a moment.

It's built over years through repetition, sacrifice, and weight carried when no one's watching.

Here's what it looks like:

- It lives in the **night-shift nurse** who carried thousands of patients through their most vulnerable hours year after year with steady hands, a sharp mind, and a full heart.
- It endures in the **third-grade teacher** who stayed in the same worn classroom for nearly four decades long after the

paint peeled and the budgets dried up, teaching generations to think, read, and believe.

- It shows up in the **field foreman** who didn't chase promotions but invested in his crew, building people, not just projects and holding the Standard when easier paths called out.
- It's rooted in the **farmer** who refused to walk away from failing land. Instead, he spent forty years restoring the soil, planting, rotating, and rebuilding so future generations would harvest more than dust.
- It echoes in the **veteran** who taught without lectures, just quiet discipline, patient resilience, and a steady presence that showed others what true strength looks like.
- It holds firm in the **civil engineer** who didn't just pave roads. She redesigned broken systems so children, workers, and goods could move safely across towns, and she did it without headlines, awards, of applause. Just genuine stability.
- It travels with the **midwife** who crossed rivers, jungles, and war zones—delivering thousands into life, knowing that beginnings shape everything.

FINAL THOUGHT

Legacy isn't a reward. It isn't given. It isn't assigned.

It's a responsibility.

It's carried; through unseen days, through repetition, through standards that hold when it would be easier to lower them.

Most people won't notice the ones who do it right.

Not at first.
Not loud enough.
Not soon enough.

But the work will stand when noise fades.

Real legacy doesn't demand attention.

- It doesn't ask for validation.
- It moves quietly; through structures that don't collapse, through cultures that stay disciplined, through people who were built stronger because someone else carried the weight first.
- It doesn't matter if the name is remembered.
- It matters if the work survives.

Because the ones who choose to carry it, the ones who stay when it's costly, who hold the Standard without applause—are the reason anything worth protecting lasts.

Legacy isn't measured by who remembers the builder.
It's measured by what's still standing after they're gone.

CHAPTER SEVEN

With the Current

USE THE TOOLS THAT AMPLIFY, NOT ERODE

This chapter isn't about pushing harder. It's about designing better.

Anyone who's tried to build something meaningful, whether it's a team, a family, a business, or a personal comeback, knows the feeling of pushing upstream. Every step takes more effort than it should. Every decision feels heavier than it is. And even when progress happens, it comes with exhaustion, not momentum.

But it doesn't have to be that way.

When the right systems are in place, progress begins to flow. Decisions get clearer. Margin returns. Time opens. Energy renews. And most importantly, the effort stops eroding and starts compounding.

But even with the right tools, there's one truth that can't be ignored:

*If what you're building doesn't create real value,
no amount of hard work will carry it.*

You can have the sharpest tools and the strongest work ethic but if you're offering something people don't need, it won't stick.

A flawless product doesn't matter if it's in the wrong place, solving the wrong thing, or showing up at the wrong time.

You're not just building. You're aligning.

The tools in this chapter are built to remove resistance. But they won't fix irrelevance. That part has to be confronted early and honestly.

Once that's clear, these tools become a force multiplier.

This chapter is broken into two parts:

1. **Operational Tools** that eliminate resistance in your daily system
2. **Leadership Tools** that multiply effort without burning out

These aren't loud tools. They won't show up in a highlight reel. But when used with discipline, they don't just make the work easier, they make it *matter*.

And they make it *last*.

PART 1: OPERATIONAL TOOLS

Financial Understanding & Discipline

The first system that frees you or holds you back.

Before someone tries to scale their effort, they need to understand the friction working against it. And for most people, whether they're leading a company or managing a household that friction starts with money.

Not because they're bad with it. But because the entire system is designed to pull it away from them.

We live in a culture that trains people to chase comfort, status, and validation. To buy the image instead of build the foundation. And slowly, they trade their independence for a payment plan. They lose margin, then freedom, then clarity until even the smallest decisions feel heavy.

And the saddest part? Most of them think it's normal.

But it's not. It's just common. And it's not the way forward.

Financial understanding is not a luxury. It's not advanced.

- It's not reserved for CEOs or finance majors.
- It's basic structure. It's movement. It's flow.

And it does more than manage dollars; it changes how people lead, how they respond to pressure, and how confidently they can take their next step.

The numbers don't need to be big. But they need to be known.

Because when someone gets their money under control, they stop reacting and start building. They shift from making desperate choices to deliberate ones. They stop asking, "Can I afford it?" and start asking, "Does it deserve my time?"

Financial clarity helps you:

- Spend with intent
- Save with clarity
- Build with discipline
- Reclaim your time, options, and peace

When the numbers align, so does the direction.
And when the money flows with purpose, the rest of the system starts to flow with it.

Cash is Oxygen: Protect It

Earn it with discipline. Protect it with purpose.

Cash doesn't just show up. It has to be earned.
And that process almost never starts with a product and it always starts with a skill.

For most people, the first phase is simple:

**Learn something useful. Do good work.
Do it with integrity even if the pay is small.**

The goal in the beginning isn't to get rich. It's to get moving. To stop waiting for the perfect opportunity and start building real value, even if it's unglamorous at first.

The rule is this:

Learn more. Earn more. Repeat.

The more useful someone becomes, the more value they create. And the more value they create, the more income they attract.

But when the income starts coming in, that's where most people lose it, because they start upgrading everything except their discipline.

The smartest ones stay frugal. They protect their cash like oxygen. They don't let comfort creep in and choke out their margin.

Because cash, once earned, is only powerful if it's protected.

And protecting it isn't complex:

- Track it weekly; like checking a pulse.
- Forecast it monthly; like reading the road ahead.
- Ask the hard questions early; before the leaks become losses.

Cash gives people space. And space gives people options. Without it, even the right path feels tight. With it, the system breathes and so does the person who runs it.

Revenue Alone is a Distraction

Not everything fast is forward.

It's easy to confuse momentum with meaning.

The numbers go up. The calendar fills. The pace increases.

And suddenly, it feels like things are working because revenue is growing.

But just because something is moving doesn't mean it's building. Revenue alone is just noise if it isn't tied to value, margin, and long-term vision.

This is where many people drift off course:

- They finally figure out how to bring in money and now they chase it wherever it appears.
- Every opportunity becomes a yes.
- Every new request gets squeezed in.
- Every dollar becomes the mission.

They start saying yes to survive. But survival slowly becomes strategy and that's when growth gets replaced by noise.

The original direction fades. Focus turns reactive. And the work becomes heavier, not better.

Because not all income is good income. Some of it comes at the cost of time, health, peace, or purpose.

And when that happens, the current turns against them and they end up working twice as hard just to stay in place.

The question isn't, "How much did I make?" The question is:

- Was it worth it?
- Is it sustainable?
- Does this move me in the right direction, or just keep me busy?

Fast revenue can feel urgent.
But only meaningful work creates lasting momentum.

Momentum without direction doesn't just stall, it pulls everything off course.

Margins are Your Early Warning System

Whatever you're building, margin tells you how much room you actually have.

Margin isn't a corporate concept. It applies everywhere.

- In business, it's profit.
- In a household, it's savings.
- For a coder, it's the extra hours to fix a crash.
- For a leader, it's the bandwidth to absorb pressure without passing it down.

Whatever the role, margin is what keeps the system from snapping.

And when it starts shrinking, it's not just about pressure. It's about control.

Because when margin disappears, someone else starts making the decisions for you.

This is where people start spiraling.

- They take every job.
- Say yes to everything.
- Burn cash, time and energy just to stay afloat.

And by the time they realize the system's failing, the problem's been there for months.

**You don't need a breakdown to make a correction.
You just need to stop pretending it's fine.**

Margin tells the truth early.

It shows you the pressure points before they explode.

And it gives you space to move when things get tight.

Don't wait for chaos to confirm the signal.

Check the margin. Adjust early. Or prepare to rebuild.

Invest Wisely, Not Emotionally

If it doesn't serve the mission, it's just noise with a price tag.

Every system has limited resources; money, time, energy, focus. And how those get allocated determines whether the effort compounds or collapses.

Smart investing isn't just about money. It's about decisions. Where you put your attention. Where you put your people. Where you put your risk.

And the line is simple:

**If it doesn't serve the mission,
it doesn't deserve the investment.**

This is where people start drifting:

- They spend to feel better.
- They upgrade because they're tired.
- They chase tools, tech, gear, and glam but none of it fixes the real problem.

If discipline doesn't come before the decision, the return will always disappoint.

Emotion is not a strategy.

Emotion says yes to anything that feels good in the moment.

Discipline waits, filters, and asks the hard questions:

- Will this move me forward?
- Will this reduce friction in the system?
- Will this help build, protect, or multiply what actually matters?

If the answer is no, it's not an investment. It's a distraction with a receipt.

And distractions don't just slow you down.

They drain the system and make you think you're making progress.

Financial Red Flags Worth Stopping For

Don't call it momentum if it's just motion with no return.

There's a difference between being busy and being effective.
If the inputs are up, but the results aren't, then something's off.
And pushing harder won't fix it.

These are red flags worth stopping for:

- Income is up. But you're still broke.
- Hours are up. But progress isn't.
- You're carrying more but not getting ahead.
- The revenue looks good but the margin keeps shrinking.
- You're busy all the time but nothing's compounding.

That's not growth. That's drift.

These are the signs of a system misaligned.

It doesn't mean everything's broken.
But it does mean something is.

The discipline here is simple:

**Don't normalize broken. Don't outrun bad math.
Don't call noise progress.**

When these flags show up:

- Stop.
- Recalculate.
- Adjust early.

Because if you wait until it collapses, you're no longer leading.

You're just cleaning up.

Backlog = Commitments

If you've already said yes to everything, don't be surprised when there's no room left for what matters.

People think backlog only applies to businesses.
It doesn't. It applies to everyone.

Your backlog is whatever you've already committed to; whether that's jobs, meetings, calls, clients, errands, responsibilities, favors, or distractions.

And if that list is packed with the wrong stuff, your time, money, and energy are already spent before the next opportunity even shows up.

The problem isn't always capacity. It's what's filling it.

You don't need to do everything.
You need to protect room for the right things.

So here's the filter:

- Is this work worth doing?
- Does this move the system forward or just keep it alive?
- Would you still say yes if you had to do it again today?

If not, it's backlog without return.

Build your calendar like you'd build your finances:

Trim the waste.
Kill the noise.
And stop saying yes to things that don't help you scale.

Because how you spend your time **is** how you spend your life.

A full schedule isn't a sign of discipline.
It's often a sign of poor filtering.

Final Thought

The numbers don't lie. The pattern doesn't change. You either adjust early or clean up later.

Everything in this section has one purpose: to keep the system aligned.
Not just financially. Structurally as well.

These tools aren't about wealth. They're about:

- Margin.
- Clarity under pressure.
- Building something that doesn't collapse every time life gets unpredictable.

If the cash is leaking, fix it.
If the margin is shrinking, protect it.
If the return isn't there, stop pretending it will be.

Discipline isn't just how you earn.

- It's how you filter.
- How you spend.
- How you decide what's worth carrying forward.

These tools won't solve everything.
But if they're used with consistency, they'll keep you in control when everything else gets loud.

That's how you stay with the current.
And that's how you build something that lasts.

PART 2: LEADERSHIP TOOLS

You can't carry the weight alone. And you're not supposed to.

The first half of this chapter was about systems: financial tools, margin, discipline, and clarity.

But systems don't scale unless people do.
And the more a mission grows, the more pressure gets transferred from what you manage to **who you build**.

You can only carry so much on your own.
That's not a weakness. That's reality.

At some point, the question isn't "Can I do this?"
It's "Who else can carry this with me?"

That's where leadership tools come in.

This section isn't about delegation. It's about multiplication.

- How to develop people who don't just fill roles, but carry standards.
- How to protect culture as you grow.
- How to lead when you're no longer close to every decision.

- And how to know when it's time to let go and how to do it without losing everything you built.

Because if the people you lead aren't growing, your system isn't scaling.

It's just getting heavier.

Build Leaders, Not Dependents

If you're the only one who can fix it, you're not leading. You're hoarding.

Real leadership isn't about being the hero.
It's about building people who don't need one.

If every problem flows back to one person, that's not strength. It's a bottleneck.

And bottlenecks don't scale. They burn out.
They get resentful. They blame others for not stepping up, even though they never gave them the space to.

This is where a lot of organizations stall:

- They say they want leaders, but they build systems that keep people dependent.
- They coach with control instead of trust.
- They reward obedience instead of initiative.
- And they confuse loyalty with silence.

But the job of a leader is to multiply, not just direct.

You build people by:

- Teaching the Standard.
- Giving them room to think.
- Letting them carry real weight.
- Letting them fail without punishment and grow without permission.

It takes more effort up front.
It's slower at first.

But it's the only way to stop fighting the system and start scaling it.

Because the moment someone else can step in and hold the Standard without you, that's not a threat.

That's proof you led them right.

Succession isn't Leaving. It's Multiplying.

Letting go isn't the end. It's the test.

Succession doesn't start when you step away.
It starts the moment you build someone who can carry part of the weight without you.

Most people think succession means walking away. It doesn't.

- It means stepping back far enough for someone else to step forward.
- And it means doing that **before** you're forced to.

If you wait until the system depends entirely on you, you didn't build a team. You built a trap.

Strong systems aren't afraid of successors.
They require them.

Because leadership isn't about being the only one who can solve it.

It's about building people who can think, decide, and act in alignment with the Standard, even when you're not in the room.

So start early.

Look for:

- Hunger
- Integrity
- Curiosity

Give space. Don't just train for technical skill; train for judgment.

Let them lead small things so they can carry bigger things later. And when they're ready, get out of the way.

Succession isn't a threat to your legacy.

It's the evidence of one.

Protecting the Culture as You Grow

Growth is only good if it doesn't erase what made you strong.

Culture isn't a slogan.
It's not written on the wall.
It's what people believe is expected of them when no one's watching.

And here's the hard truth:
As soon as a team grows, culture starts drifting.

The proximity fades. The tone gets diluted.

And if no one's paying attention, the very thing that made the work sharp starts getting replaced with noise.

That's not a maybe. That's automatic.
And unless someone's protecting it, **it's gone.**

Here's how strong leaders protect it:

1. Choose People Who Guard the Standard

You're not just hiring skill.
You're hiring influence.

Every new person either reinforces the culture or dilutes it.

Look for:

- Alignment with the values
- Humility in execution
- Accountability when pressure hits

You're not just adding labor. You're shaping the environment. Choose accordingly.

2. Write Down What Was Once Understood

Early on, culture spreads through proximity.
But that doesn't scale.

What used to be absorbed needs to be taught.
Write it down. Define it. Teach it.

- What matters
- What's non-negotiable
- How decisions should feel

Don't assume anyone gets it just because you said it once.

3. Give the Front Line a Voice

Culture lives where the work happens.
If the people closest to the pressure feel ignored, culture decays.

Create feedback loops that actually get used.
Listen without ego.
Act when it counts.

4. Move Fast When Culture is at Risk

Toxicity doesn't always scream.
Sometimes it just lingers; quiet, cynical, corrosive.

If someone erodes trust, they can't stay.

Not because they're bad, but because the Standard matters more than any one person.

Move fast when risk arises. And make sure people know why.

5. Model It Every Day

You are the culture.

What you do gets copied.
What you tolerate becomes normal.
And what you reinforce, good or bad, gets multiplied.

Show up sharp. Be consistent.
Protect the tone as if the system depends on it, because it does.

Steward What You've Been Given

If someone chooses to follow you, take it seriously. That trust isn't free.

Leadership isn't a title. It's a loan.

Every time someone chooses to follow you, whether it's for a shift, a project, or a season, they're giving you something valuable:

- Their time
- Their trust
- Their energy

They could give it to anyone. They chose to give it to you.
And that means you owe them something back.

You owe them clarity.

Make it clear what matters.

Set expectations. Re-set them when needed.

No one thrives in confusion.

You owe them feedback.

Not just when things go wrong. Not once a year.
Give it consistently.

If they're slipping, tell them.
If they're crushing it, say so.

Silence doesn't protect people. It blindsides them.

You owe them consistency.

No landmines.

No mood swings.

Show up steady. People trust what they can predict.

You owe them your time.

Not all of it, but enough to teach, coach, and listen.
If you're too busy to develop people, you're not leading.

You're just managing throughput.

You owe them protection.

From chaos. From burnout.

From toxicity.

Clear the road so they can actually run.

You owe them honesty.

Even when it's uncomfortable. Even when it makes you look bad.
People can handle the truth. What they can't handle is pretending.

Leadership is earned. Every day.

Protect what you're carrying and never forget who gave it to you.

Before You Quit, Check the Drift

Most people don't quit all at once. They fade. Quietly. Slowly.

Quitting doesn't always start loud.

- It starts as silence.
- As detachment.
- As low energy.
- As "I just need a break."

And by the time someone says, "I'm done," the drift has been happening for a while.

If you're thinking about quitting, here's what to check first:

Check what's actually weighing you down.

Before you call it burnout, check the basics:

- Are you getting enough sleep?
- Are you overcommitted?
- Are you working in circles and spending effort in the wrong place?
- Are you carrying someone else's weight?

Most people don't quit because they're weak.
They quit because they've been running at full speed with no clarity, no support, and no room to breathe.

You don't fix that by walking away.
You fix it by being honest about what's broken and correcting it while you still have the chance.

Don't misdiagnose the pressure.

Sometimes we blame the job, the client, or the schedule, when the real issue is somewhere else entirely.

- A relationship is strained.

- Health is slipping.
- The right people aren't close anymore.
- There's no space to breathe.

It's easier to blame the part of your life that's closest. But don't blow up the right thing just because something else is off. ***Don't let other people's actions change your purpose.***

You'll be undervalued.
You'll be overlooked.
You'll carry more than your share and still get less credit.

That's not a reason to quit. That's a reason to recenter.

Adjust? Yes.
Quit? Not yet.

FINAL WORD:

Before you walk away, pause.

- If you're tired, rest.
- If you're frustrated, reset.
- If you're overwhelmed, simplify.

But if there's still a spark, protect it.

Because if you made it this far, you weren't built to quit. **You were built to carry weight.**

And you're not done yet.

———○———

CHAPTER EIGHT

This is Where You Can't Fake It

This chapter is where the talk ends. Where pressure strips away the polish. Where shortcuts show up dressed as strategy and real leadership either holds or folds. Every moment in here is pulled from real tension, real teams, and real consequences.

Here, the Custodian Standard and Core Commitments stop being ideas and start being actions. These aren't hypotheticals. They're field tests. The kind of moments where doing the right thing isn't easy, clean, or obvious. But it still has to be done.

Grouped by theme, these scenarios are the gut checks of leadership.

SECTION 1: STRENGTHENING TEAM DYNAMICS

1. When the Team Isn't Clicking

Lesson: Respect is the floor. Integrity is non-negotiable.

Years ago, I was the engineer on a fast-moving, high-stakes project. From the outside, it looked like we were doing okay, we were about 60% on time and 35% on budget. But from the inside? It was a mess.

The team was filled with people who were more focused on protecting their own image than pushing the project forward.

The culture was off. Conversations were shallow. Accountability was blurry. Everyone was rowing, but at a different beat. And the project manager? He never should've been in that seat.

After watching the first 15 months of the job get squandered, I'd had enough. I wasn't going to let the rest of it collapse. That Friday night, I met with my senior PM and gave him a list of five names. People I had identified as the real drag on the job. Some were blocking decisions. Some were dragging their feet. Some were just there for the check.

My message was simple:

Remove them from the project, or I'm out.

If I'm involved in something, I'm not going to let it fail.
And I'm not going to let dead weight sink the team.

He heard me. He talked with the area manager that weekend. By Sunday, we were back in a room. He looked me in the eye and said, "They'll either be reassigned or removed. We'll evaluate if there's any value we can still get from them; but either way, they're off this job."

I had one final ask:

If the project manager stays, I don't want him talking to me.

Period. That line was drawn too. And they honored that.

All five were reassigned. The dead weight cleared out.

And the shift was immediate.

We started moving. The team clicked. The tension left the room.

Everyone got in rhythm.

It was a race to the finish and we made it. On time. Clean.

Here's the truth:

- You don't have to like each other.
- But you do have to **respect** the work.
- You do have to **protect** the team.

And you can't let dysfunction stay just because it's easier than addressing it.

***You* are the culture.**
Not the logo. Not the handbook.
You decide what's tolerated and what's not.

Respect is the floor.
Execution is the expectation.
Integrity is the non-negotiable.

Everything else?
Leave it outside.

2. Protect the Ones with Heart

Lesson: Heart can't be taught. Skill can.

I was a project manager on a job many years ago, and like most projects, we had laborers out in the field. Two of them were young, barely got noticed. Technically, they didn't report to me. Not even close. But they were on my site, and I watched them.

They showed up early. Worked hard. Asked questions and acted like they were willing to learn anything and everything.

And I couldn't shake the thought:

These two had heart. Real heart.

No one was going to promote them. No one was tracking their potential. But I saw it.

So I pulled them from the field and brought them into the office.

We didn't even have a position for what I wanted them to do. So I flipped through the HR manual until I found a title: "Construction Technician."

Nobody in the company had ever used it for a real hire. So I made it up for them.

We trained them to support the superintendent. To help the engineers. To organize the details that everyone else kept dropping. It was chaos at first. Slow. Messy. A total learning curve.

But they stuck with it. And so did I.

Fast forward a couple years and both were well on their way to becoming project engineers. No degrees. No traditional path. Just grit, coaching, and belief.

And today? Both are thriving. Still in the industry. Working for companies I respect.

That's what people don't always get:

- You don't protect someone because they're already great.
- You protect them because they've got the stuff that can become great.

Heart can't be taught. Skill can.

I didn't lower the bar.

I raised the floor, so they had a shot to reach it.

That's what real teams do.

Spot the quiet ones with fire in their gut and make space for them to grow.

3. Back the Ones Who Always Showed Up

Lesson: Loyalty is a two-way street.

I've had people burn out. I've had people outgrow their seat. And I've learned there's no one-size-fits-all response when someone starts to slip. But here's the line I hold:

If someone has always shown up for you, you don't walk away the second they falter.

One of my guys had been with us a long time. Solid. Loyal. But one year, he started slipping badly. His personal life was crashing, stress was bleeding into everything, and the performance wasn't there.

Everyone on my management team wanted him gone.

But I held the line. I told them straight:

> *You care about finances. I care about that person more.*

Even my business partner was frustrated. Our guy was costing us money. But I didn't care. Because this was someone who had carried the weight when we needed him.

And when someone does that, they earn something most people don't talk about: Grace.

I defended him. I backed him. I told everyone:

> *We're not cutting him loose.*

Eventually, we shifted his role. And now? He's critical. He's focused. He's delivering.

He didn't just recover; he became an asset again.

Not because we gave him a second chance.

Because we never stopped believing he earned one.

That's one kind of story.

Then there's the other kind, the ones who grow beyond the role.

I had a project manager who came to me one day and said he wanted to start his own company. He wasn't quitting. He was building.

I told him, "You should work both jobs until your business can support your salary and when it can, you come let me know. Then you leave clean."

Most leaders would've tightened the leash. I supported him.

And then COVID hit. He was relieved he still had a stable paycheck during that stretch.

But a few years later, after things picked back up, he came back to me and said, "I'm ready."

I didn't guilt him. I didn't try to keep him.

I helped him.

Now he owns his own business and I still give him work.

Because when someone leaves the right way, the door stays open.

That's what it means to back the ones who always showed up.

- Sometimes they need support.
- Sometimes they need room to leave.
- Sometimes they come back stronger.
- Sometimes they don't come back at all.

But either way, you don't lead through convenience. You lead through conviction.

And conviction means never forgetting who carried the weight when it mattered.

4. Not Everyone Wants the Title

Lesson: Excellence doesn't always need a title.

I've got a few foremen who could dance circles around some superintendents in this industry. They run clean jobs. They lead without noise. And when things get tough, they don't flinch, they double down and carry more.

Every time we've tried to promote them; they've turned us down.

Not because they're afraid. Not because they're not capable.

They just don't want the title. The meetings. The added pressure that comes with managing people who aren't built like them.

They just want to build.

To execute.

To be excellent at what they do.

And you know what? I respect that.

So we don't guilt them. We don't push. We don't use their paycheck as leverage.

We pay them like superintendents because they're worth it. And we let them keep doing what they love.

Every few years, we check in: "You want that promotion yet?"

And every few years, it's the same answer: "Not yet."

No pressure. No problem.

Because I'd rather have a master builder who wants to stay on the ground than a reluctant manager who feels like they were pushed into the wrong role.

Too many companies confuse potential with obligation.

They push people up a ladder they never asked to climb and lose the very talent they were trying to reward.

Not everyone wants to lead teams.

Some people lead through example.

Both matter.

- So you build around them.
- You support their path, not your plan.
- You honor mastery, even if it never comes with a title.

Because great teams aren't built on hierarchy alone.

They're built on clarity, trust, and space for different kinds of greatness.

5. No Room for Games

Lesson: Politics is a tax strong teams don't pay.

You can hear it before you see it.

- The subtle positioning.
- The silence that's not neutral.
- The energy shift from outcomes to optics.

People stop focusing on the work. They start managing perception.

Conversations get calculated.
Credit becomes currency.

And trust starts leaking out the edges.

This is how politics creeps in.

And if you don't cut it early, it spreads.

Progress slows.
Meetings turn into theater.
Teams protect turf instead of pushing the mission.

High-performance cultures don't survive that kind of rot.

- They don't let titles outrank truth.
- They don't reward noise over results.

So the response?

Quiet. Direct. Fast.

Pull the players aside.
Say it clearly:

This team runs on responsibility, not politics.

If they adjust, great.
If they don't, move around them.
No drama. No announcements. Just action.

Because position doesn't matter.
Performance does.

Drama slows the mission. Discipline keeps it moving.

6. When No One Speaks Up

Lesson: Silence isn't discipline; sometimes it's a warning.

The work is moving.
But the team is silent.

No feedback.
No pushback.
No ideas, just quiet compliance.

At first, it might look like discipline.
But it's not.

It's a warning sign.

Because when people stop speaking up,

They stop thinking ahead.

They stop flagging problems.
They stop solving things before they break.
And eventually, they do break.

That silence has a cause.
Sometimes it's someone hiding mistakes.
But more often, it's fear.

Fear of being blamed.
Fear of being dismissed.
Fear of being punished for telling the truth.

That's when leadership has to lean in, not back.

It starts with presence:
- Show up.
- Ask real questions.
- Actually listen.

Make it clear:

Speaking up doesn't get you punished. It gets you respected.

And if someone on the team is creating that fear, whether
a toxic lead, a dismissive manager, a broken system,
it gets handled. Fast.

Because a quiet team won't catch the problem until it's too late.

And by then, the cost isn't just the mistake.
It's the trust that was lost with it.

Strong teams speak up and strong leaders make sure their teams
know they can without paying a price for it.

7. You Can't Treat Everyone the Same

Lesson: Uniform Standard, customized delivery.

This one isn't about someone I led.

It's about someone who had to lead me.

Early in my career, I was harsh. I delivered the message like a robot. I didn't care how it landed.

I thought if I was right, that was enough.
Didn't matter how someone felt, just whether they got the point.

And I roughed up a lot of people because of it.

Eventually, my senior PM; who is still one of my mentors currently, pulled me into his office.

He looked me straight in the eye and said;

"You're one of the smartest people I've worked with. But also, not that smart."

Because if you were really smart, you'd know how to deliver a message based on who's receiving it."

He didn't yell. He didn't embarrass me.

It wasn't a compliment. It wasn't a takedown.

It was customized correction and it hit hard.

I left his office that day not knowing whether I'd just been praised or wrecked.

But over time, I figured it out: he had delivered the truth in a way that I could actually hear it.

That moment changed everything.

Now I tell others the same thing he told me.

And I coach with the same approach he used on me.

Because leadership isn't about being loud.

It's about being clear and effective.

- Some people need direct feedback.
- Some need space.
- Some need coaching.
- Some need a walk, not a speech.

But too many leaders use the same tone, the same method, for everyone.

It doesn't work.

- Same job title doesn't mean same wiring.
- Same standard doesn't mean same style.

Great leaders adjust, not to coddle, but to connect.

Not to soften the message, but to make sure it lands.

Yes, the bar stays high.
But how you coach someone to reach it?

That's where leadership lives.

Uniform Standard.
Customized delivery.

That's how real teams grow.

8. The Cost of Weak Habits

Lesson: A team is only as strong as its weakest habits.

We once took a job we shouldn't have touched. It was outside our usual geographic area, and the only reason we said yes was because we had a commitment from a superintendent and a few crews who said they'd run with it.

But once we got going, it started falling apart.

Deadlines slipped. Corners got cut. Excuses became the norm. It wasn't one big failure; it was a hundred small ones stacked on top of each other. And the more we tried to correct it—meetings, conversations, second chances—the clearer it became: we weren't going to get alignment.

They weren't bad people. They just weren't wired for our Standard.

So I made the call: let them all go.

Believe me, I don't like firing people. That's never my first move.

But when it becomes clear we're not going to get alignment, I owe it to the rest of the team and the company to protect what we've built.

We still had to deliver the project. So we leaned on our inner circle, the people we trusted, and made it happen. It took everything. It was draining. And it put stress on the whole company. But we got it done the right way.

Here's what that experience taught me:

Weak habits don't stay isolated. They spread.

The moment you let "almost" pass for "done," the whole job shifts. The tone drops. Pride fades. And before long, sloppiness becomes the new normal.

So when you see that drift happening, you don't wait. You tighten the work.

- You raise the bar directly, clearly, unapologetically.
- You bring in sharper habits.
- You reward precision.
- You make "close enough" uncomfortable again.

Because sloppiness isn't just about the task.

It's a signal of what the team believes is okay.

And if the Standard really matters?

Then "almost" doesn't cut it.

SECTION 2: MAKING STRATEGIC DECISIONS

9. The Work You Don't Take

Lesson: Turning down bad work is an excellent strategy, fear is a bad strategy.

Years ago, I turned down a project I really needed.

I mean, I really needed it. We had a bunch of people, and we didn't have any work at all.

It was a bridge and wall job. Good size, decent margins on paper. And we were hungry for work at the time. But something in the contract didn't sit right. They wanted the subcontractor to carry all the material risk, without allowing any markup on those materials. Worse, they picked the suppliers themselves, negotiated the prices, and told us to just bake it into our bid. Then they'd deduct those material costs from our payout, with no approval, no questions, no accountability.

I couldn't shake a bad feeling:

- The supplier had no reason to bill correctly, knowing there was no real control or pushback.
- The general contractor had no reason to question it, because they weren't the ones paying.
- And we were the ones left holding the bag. **So I walked.**

People said I was being too cautious. That we needed the job. But I've learned: if the numbers look good but the terms don't feel right, trust the feeling.

Later, I watched multiple subcontractors go bankrupt working under that same structure.

But that wasn't a one-time decision.

Throughout the life of the company, I've probably turned down two out of every three jobs we've negotiated. Not because we couldn't perform, but because the deal had to make sense for our strategy, not the general contractor's.

And I'll be honest; we haven't always gotten it right.

There have been a couple jobs we accepted that were completely outside our geographic area. On paper, they looked manageable. But they were tough to deliver and definitely not profitable. We didn't quit; we finished every bit of work. But we paid the price. And we learned another the lesson: **don't stretch yourself just to say yes.**

We don't take pride in walking away. We take pride in knowing what to walk away from.

Because saying no to the wrong job doesn't slow you down.

- It keeps you in business.
- It protects your team.
- And over time, it's how you win for real.

10. Pause Before You Commit

Lesson: Real decisions deserve discipline, not speed.

I've been in this position hundreds of times.

- The room's tense.
- The clock's loud.
- Everyone's looking at me for the answer.

And I **pause.**

I've done it so often my team gave it a name, "The Jaber Pause."

It's not a stall.
It's not hesitation.
It's discipline.

Because when the pressure is on and everyone wants a quick "yes," that's exactly when you slow down.

I've learned the hard way:

- Speed looks like strength but sometimes it's just insecurity wearing confidence.
- Reacting quickly might win the room.
- But it can lose the project, the client, the whole mission.

I've seen bad hires happen because no one paused.

I've seen teams burn out because leaders overcommitted.

I've watched partnerships implode because someone wanted to look decisive instead of being disciplined.

So now, when my gut says "Wait," I listen.

I step back.
I find the missing piece.
I map the risk.
I make sure we're not walking into something we can't carry.

That pause has saved us more times than I can count.

- It's not fear.
- It's clarity.

Because reacting is easy.

Leading means slowing things down long enough to see clearly.

When the decision is finally ready, I don't flinch.

- I move sharp.
- I move clean.

Because the choice earned it.

11. Too High, Too Low; It's Still a Problem

Lesson: Protect the Standard on both sides of the deal.

Years ago, when I was still an engineer, we got a quote for a material item that didn't make sense. It looked high, way too high. On top of that, the supplier wanted escalation protection. But when I looked into it, I realized it was just steel pipe, cut into 6-foot sections. That's all it was.

So I dug in.

I researched the specs, started calling around, and eventually found a foundry in Alabama that sold the same pipe, but only in 42-foot lengths. That was fine. I called a metal workshop that could cut them to size, worked out the logistics, and got the shipment delivered to them. They cut it down, we paid them for the work, and we brought the material to the jobsite.

The total cost? A quarter of what the original supplier wanted and before they even applied their price hike.

I wasn't trying to be clever. I was protecting the company.

Years later, I was on the other side—as a business owner.

We got a quote from a subcontractor that seemed way too low. I don't share numbers with anyone. That's a rule I live by. But I know the owner who sent that quote and I knew if I signed it, he'd honor it. He would've taken the hit quietly. Most people would've seen that as a win.

But I called him.

I told him to double-check his numbers. That something felt off.

He called me back and said, "Yeah, we found the error."

He sent a revised quote; not just to me, but to everyone.

But he gave us the best number; because we were the only ones who told him the truth.

We won the job.
And we still work with that sub today.

Because that's what trust looks like in real time.

Here's the point:

If the number doesn't make sense.
Trust your gut.Ask. Check. Speak up.

Because the best operators don't just chase value.

They protect the Standard.

On both sides of the deal.

> *Don't assume.*
> *Don't manipulate.*
> *Don't stay quiet just to win.*

Because you might win the job and lose the relationship.

And over time? That's more expensive than any bid.

12. The Price of Your Name

Lesson: Leadership starts with how you carry your name.

Early in my career, I was reviewing invoices from a vendor, just a routine task. Check the numbers, approve the cost, move on.

One month, a vendor submitted an invoice that was way lower than it should've been. It was a mistake on their side. Most people would've seen it, shrugged, and called it a win for the budget.

But not me.

I recalculated it, corrected it to the exact amount they had earned, and sent it back.

No announcement. No recognition. Just one simple rule I lived by:

**If my name is going on it, it has to be right.
Not a penny more. Not a penny less.**

My boss at the time noticed.

He asked, "Why are you paying people more than they asked for?"

I told him: "Because they earned it. And if it were the other way around, I'd be just as quick to correct it. Integrity doesn't run in one direction."

I didn't think much about it after that. I just did what was right.

Years passed. That same vendor and I eventually started a company together.

And only years after we were already in business, **after trust had already been built quietly over time**, he told me:

"I never told you this before, but that day? That was the moment I knew that one day, we're going to work together. Because honesty like that… it stays with you."

And it did.

Because people always remember how you carry your name.

Even when they say nothing. Even when you think no one's watching. Because someone always is.

Leadership doesn't start with your title.

It starts with what you sign. What you approve. What you ignore or refuse to.

And that Standard? It didn't stay in that moment:

**It's still what we practice at our company
and what we hold our people to.**

13. Growth Won't Kill You. Greed Will

Lesson: More isn't better. Better is better.

You'll hit that moment; if you haven't already.

- Momentum kicks in.
- The big opportunity lands.
- Everything looks wide open.

And people start saying,

"Now's the time. Go faster. Scale it."

But growth only works if your foundation is ready.

Growth won't kill you. Greed will.

A person can survive without food for weeks.

Try to swallow too much at once? You choke.

Same goes for businesses. Same goes for teams. Same goes for you.

Most people don't collapse because they're doing too little.

They collapse because they try to do too much, too fast.

To say yes before you're ready.
To add weight without structure.
To chase scale without clarity.

And that's how people burn out. How great work turns sloppy. How momentum becomes damage.

So before you say yes, ask yourself:

- Can I carry this without snapping?
- Is my system built to hold this?
- Will this stretch me, or wreck me?

If the answer isn't clear, don't panic.

But don't lie to yourself either.

Slow it down.
Stabilize what's already in play.
Then grow; on purpose.

Because anyone can grow fast.

The ones who last are the ones who grow right.

14. The Client that Keeps Moving the Goalposts

Lesson: Document. Clarify. Protect your people.

It always starts small.

- A tweak here. An adjustment there.
- Nothing worth pushing back on, yet.
- So you let it slide.

But the changes keep coming.

Deadlines shift. Expectations blur.

And before you know it, the work looks nothing like what was agreed to.

Now your team is under pressure, burning hours, trying to meet targets no one ever signed off on.

There's no formal change in scope, just informal chaos.

- This is where most teams fold.
- They say yes to keep the peace.
- They absorb the pressure.
- They take the hit in silence and hoping it'll smooth out later.

But strong teams don't get steamrolled.

And they don't blow up the relationship either.

Stay sharp. Do three things:

1. Document everything.
2. Ask for clear direction.
3. Spell out the impact every time.

This isn't about being difficult.

It's about being clear.

When it's time to speak up, you do it calm and direct.

- You protect your people.
- You defend the work.
- You negotiate with facts, not frustration.

And when the other side owns their part? Meet them halfway.

Compromise when it's earned, not assumed.

Because most of the time, it's not bad intent.

It's just a bad process.

And bad process is manageable:
As long as both sides carry the cost.

As for court? Avoid it if you can.

Not because you're scared to fight.

But because in that fight?

Only the lawyers win.

15. If You Have to Force It, It's Probably Not Worth It

Lesson: Know when to push and when to walk.

You've been taught to push through everything.

> *To grind.*
> *To power forward.*
> *To carry weight no matter what.*

And most of the time, that's right.

But not always.

There's a difference between pushing yourself when it's hard and forcing something that was never aligned to begin with.

I've lived this one the hard way.

I once walked away from something massive, something fully built, paid for, and expected; because deep down, I knew it wasn't right. It wasn't emotional. It wasn't dramatic. It was clear. We weren't aligned. And no matter how much time, money, or pride had been spent, I wasn't going to fake it just to save face.

I didn't flinch. But that didn't make it easy.

- The cost was high. Not just for me but for everyone around me.
- I wish I had made the call sooner.

But the Standard held and I've never once regretted honoring it.

And that's my point.

You might be carrying something right now; a deal, a job, a relationship, a partnership—

and the only reason you're still in it is because you've already spent too much to let it go.

But you know it doesn't fit. You know you're faking alignment.

You know it's not going to fix itself.

Push when it's right- but hard.
Walk when it's broken and pretending won't fix it.

Leadership means knowing the difference.

It means choosing clarity, even when the price is steep.

Because forcing something past the point of truth?

That's not strength. That's delay.

So yes, dig deeper.

- Push when it matters.
- Fight for what deserves it.

But if your gut tells you, it's not right?

Believe it.

Decide early.

And move on.

SECTION 3: ACCOUNTABILITY IN MOTION

16. When the Blame Starts Flying

Lesson: Clarity fixes more than blame ever will.

When things go sideways, plans fall apart, timelines slip, pressure builds, everyone starts looking for someone to blame.

The manager blames the team.

The team blames the tools.

Someone blames the client.

And the client? They just want answers. Fast.

But blame doesn't fix anything.

Clarity does.

Your job in that moment isn't to react.

It's to step back and ask the right questions:

- Were expectations clear?
- Was someone stretched too thin?
- Was this a one-time error or a system problem?

You listen, not for noise, but for truth.

Then you lead. You adjust the plan. You bring in support.

You fix what failed, without throwing anyone under the bus.

Because when trust breaks, the work breaks.

And strong teams can survive pressure.

But they can't survive blame culture.

So when the room gets loud, stay calm.

**When the fingers point, stay focused.
And when everyone's protecting themselves,
protect the truth.**

That's what leadership does.

Not by blaming. By leading.

17. "When It's on You," Own It.

Lesson: Ownership of one mistake creates oxygen for the team.

You won't always get it right.

Sometimes the miss is yours.

- You made the call.
- You moved too fast.
- You overlooked a red flag.
- You backed the wrong plan or the wrong person.

And now the cost is real.

Deadlines are slipping.

Tension is rising.

The team is quiet, but they all feel it.

They're waiting to see who's going to name it.

That moment? That's the test.

You don't wait for someone else to call it out.

You own it; fully, clearly, and fast.

> *"That's on me. Here's how we fix it."*

Not to look noble. Not to score points.

But to steady the room.

Because when you dodge accountability, the whole team feels it.

- They go silent.
- They stop raising issues.
- They start covering themselves instead of solving the problem.

But when you step up, clean and without spin, you flip the tone.

- You create breathing room.
- You shift focus from blame to solution.
- You get things moving again.

This doesn't mean you take the blame for everything.

It means you take responsibility when it's yours—and carry it like a leader.

Ownership doesn't break you.

- It builds trust.
- It protects the Standard.
- And it sets the tone for what comes next.

Because real leadership doesn't come from being perfect:

**It comes from being accountable
when it matters most.**

18. The Crisis that Hits on a Weekend

Lesson: Leadership contains urgency, not spreads it.

It always shows up at the worst time.

Friday night. Holiday morning.

When everyone's finally off the clock and the system should be running smooth.

- Then something breaks.

- Something goes sideways.
- And suddenly, all eyes are on you.

This is where most people panic.

They flood the group chat.

They loop everyone in, not to solve it, but to be seen reacting.

But that's not leadership. That's noise.

When it hits, you stay calm.

You assess the situation.

You loop in only the people who are truly needed.

You act with clarity, not adrenaline.

And unless it's truly critical, you protect your team's time.

You don't reward urgency with chaos.

You don't drag the whole crew into the fire just because something needs fixing.

You carry the weight. Quietly. Deliberately.

This is why you build systems.

This is why you build trust.

So that when things go wrong, you already know who to call, what to check, and what not to blow out of proportion.

Leadership doesn't panic.

Doesn't spread the urgency.

Contains it.

Leadership absorbs pressure, so the rest of the team doesn't have to.

19. When the Storm Hit Everything

Lesson: Build the bench before the storm hits.

Sometimes everything breaks at once.

Projects stall. Jobs fall apart. Delays stack. Clients disappear.

And if that storm hits while you're strong, you fight through it.

But if it hits while you're on empty?

That's where the truth shows up.

I've lived through that moment.

It was right after I ended a long-term relationship, already emotionally drained, already mentally scattered. I was making bad decisions. I was distracted. And then everything started going sideways at work.

One job got canceled by the owner. Another was pulled. Two more got delayed. One fell apart completely.

Five major hits, **all within two months.**

And I had nothing in me to fight it.

> *I wasn't helpful to my team.*
> *I wasn't showing up for my partner.*
> *I wasn't leading anyone, not even myself.*

But my team did what I couldn't.

They didn't panic.

They didn't point fingers.

They stepped up and navigated the company through the storm, until I could wake up and steer again.

And yes; it cost us.

We lost real money. We took real damage.
But we made it. And we came out stronger.

Because that's what saved us: **We had a bench.**

Leadership culture had already been built.

Systems were already in place.

People already knew what the Standard was, even without me in the room.

And that's the part that matters most:

- You won't always be at your best.
- Life will hit you. Business will break.
- And when both happen at the same time you'll need more than your own strength.

So build the bench.

Train people who don't wait for you to tell them what to do.

Build culture that holds and even when you don't.

Because one day, everything will shake and the captain won't be at the wheel.

Make sure the ship still floats.

20. Leadership in the Red

Lesson: Real leadership shows up when it hurts.

Sometimes the work ends, but the people don't.

- The projects stall. The cash dries up.
- But your team still shows up. Still trusting. Still waiting to see what you're going to do.

And that's when the weight hits.

You don't have enough revenue to justify keeping everyone on.

But you've got too much loyalty, too much history, to let them go.

And deep down, you know: **if you cut them loose now, it's not just them you're letting down. It's you.**

I was in a rough place at the time. It was during one of the hardest personal stretches of my life and professionally, things were breaking all around me.

We had just taken a string of hits: jobs canceled, pulled, delayed, lost.

I wasn't at my best. Wasn't even close.

But one decision broke through all that noise. I said,

"We're not letting anyone go. I don't care if we don't have the work; we are paying our people."

That decision didn't come from strategy. It came from conviction.

- I wasn't about to leave hanging the people who had built this company with me.
- And as crazy as it sounds, **that one call pulled me out of my spiral.**

It gave me a reason to fight.

A sense of purpose when everything felt dim.

It reminded me that this company was never just about business, it was about people.

And those people were watching.

So we found work.

- We took a tight job with a strict budget and made it work.
- We didn't cut corners. We didn't beg.

- We delivered and it kept the team together. It gave us momentum when we needed it most.

We didn't make money on that project.

But we earned something bigger: **trust.**

Because real leadership isn't tested when things are smooth.

It's tested when the bottom of the spreadsheet turns red

and your people are still looking to you for answers.

That's when it matters.

Not when the margins are clean.

But when the pressure is real and the people are watching.

Do you fold?

Or do you carry it?

Because they won't remember the revenue.

They'll remember if you stood with them when it would've been easier and cheaper to walk away.

21. Before You Join the Excuse Team

Lesson: Excuses get easier every time. Don't start.

I was the engineer on a job with a tight deadline and one serious problem.

- It was an airport road, scheduled to open.
- But we didn't have signs.
- And no signs meant no opening.

It was late Friday. The supplier wasn't responding.

The project manager had already checked out.

The site team was drained.

Everyone was ready to chalk it up to the supply chain.

And I'll be honest, no one would've blamed us.

The excuse was clean. It was believable.

And it would've bought us time.

But I couldn't sleep.

Something about it didn't sit right with me.

So I showed up to the jobsite. In the dark.

Around 5 a.m., a guy from our QC team rolled in.

I looked at him and said, "You got the energy to drive to Little Rock?"

He said, "Sure." That's all I needed.

We jumped in the car.

I slept in the passenger seat while he drove, straight to the supplier's warehouse.

Once we got there, we walked through the warehouse ourselves.

We found the signs, finished, sitting in the queue.

I asked for the warehouse manager, told him the situation, and made it clear:

> *These signs need to be at the front of the line.*
> *First out Monday morning.*

He moved them.

We stood there while they were staged and loaded onto the next delivery truck.

By Monday afternoon, they were on-site.

We made the deadline. The road opened on time.

- No applause. No bonus. No spotlight.
- Just the job; done right.

Nobody asked me to do it. And I would've been safe doing nothing.

But here's what I know:

**Once you start making excuses,
they get easier every time.**

So I went one more round before I let that version of me start to form.

And I've never regretted it.

That's what ownership looks like. Not just doing your part:

**But doing what the moment needs,
even when no one else will.**

22. You Don't Get More Time; You Get Smarter

Lesson: Lead the situation; don't get crushed by it.

The ribbon cutting was scheduled.

- The date was printed on the invitations. The coins were already cast.
- There was no shifting anything.

And the work wasn't done.

We were subcontracted to build the cast-in-place walls on a bridge project.

But the GC delayed giving us access to the bridge so we couldn't start the walls.

By the time we were finally able to move, the window was gone. There just wasn't enough time.

It wasn't going to happen, not the way it was originally designed.

So I went straight to the segment manager.

I laid it out clearly: "This can't be built in time. Not as it stands. But here's what we can do…"

I proposed removing the wave-pattern coping from the critical path.

- Redesign the stem of the wall so we could build the core now and cast the decorative top later.
- Just give me a clean design. I'll handle the rest.

He agreed.

We moved. Fast.

- We pulled four of our best crews.
- I was there every day. So was my Technical Manager.
- We worked straight through weekends and holidays.
- No drama. No shortcuts. Just full commitment, on-site, until it was done.

Right after we started, the GC's managers called me:

"Are you going to make it?"

I still had my doubts. But my answer was simple:

"I'll let you know on the day of. But until then, we'll try like hell."

And we did.

We finished with two days to spare.

But let's be clear; **if we hadn't redesigned it, it wouldn't have worked.**

- This wasn't just about working harder.
- **It was about getting smarter.**

Because when the pressure's real, when the deadline won't move, and the coins are already minted

You don't get more time.

You rethink the sequence.

You cut what's not critical.

You lead the conversation, not just the labor.

You don't lie.

You don't panic.

You don't hide.

You get clear.

You get creative.

And you deliver.

Because that's what leadership looks like when time runs out.

You don't break.

You get smarter.

SECTION 4: LEAD OR GET OUT OF THE WAY

23. When Performance Comes with Poison

Lesson: Performance without character is a time bomb.

You'll see it eventually.

Someone on your team is getting results.

- They hit the numbers.
- They deliver.
- And on paper, they look like a star.

But underneath the surface, they're creating damage.

People are tense around them.
Morale drops.
Trust slips.

They lead with intimidation, not discipline.

And slowly, the culture around them starts to rot.

That's not leadership. That's a time bomb.

**Because performance without character
will always explode.**

And when it does, it takes good people with it.

So what do you do?

You address it.
Directly. Early. Professionally.
You give them clarity.
You show them the impact.

You give them a chance to adjust—no guessing, no surprises.

Because nobody should be blindsided.

But nobody should be protected by results, either.

If it's a bad week, you coach.

If it's a pattern, then you make the call.

- Clean. Quiet. Decisive.
- No drama. No humiliation. No dragging it out.

You don't let damage stay just because it performs.

Because the longer you protect the wrong person, the more, good people start to leave.

The numbers might look fine.
But the culture won't.
And eventually neither will the team.

24. The Standard Applies to Everyone

Lesson: No exceptions. No favorites. No excuses.

Not everyone who slows you down works for you.

Sometimes it's a subcontractor.
A vendor.
A supplier.

Someone outside your org chart, but inside your workflow.

They're not trying to fail. But they're missing the mark.

*And now **your** people are paying for **their** mistakes.*

That's when your leadership gets tested.

- You can't afford to overreact.
- But you can't afford to let it slide either.

When someone on the outside starts affecting what's happening inside, you act:

- One clear warning documented.
- Expectations reset, in writing.
- Consequences; laid out before the next move.

If it happens again? They eat the cost.

Not to punish; to protect the Standard.

Because when you tolerate failure from partners, you send a message to your team:

"The standard is flexible."

And once that message lands, everything softens.

- So you hold the line.
- Not just for your direct reports
- **For anyone touching the mission.**

Because the moment someone is part of your delivery, they're part of your Standard.

No exceptions.

No favorites.

No excuses.

25. The Standard Starts at the Start

Lesson: Pride is built into how you start.

It's easy to relax at the end.

- The checklist is done.
- The review looks clean.
- Everyone's ready to move on.

But that's not where the Standard is built.

It's built at the beginning.

You don't set the tone at the finish.

You set it from the first move.

If something feels off in the early stages, it probably is.

- Even if it checks the boxes.

- Even if no one calls it out.

Strong teams don't wait for cracks to show.

They tighten the work from day one.

Because pride doesn't get bolted on at the end.

It gets poured into the foundation.

Leadership shows up early.

- Defines what good looks like.
- Walks the work before the deadline shows up.
- That's how you build it right the first time.

Because when the mindset becomes "just get it done," that's exactly what you get: something barely done.

And when pressure returns, that's when the cracks break open.

So yes, fix what needs fixing.

But don't build on patchwork and hope no one notices.

Start sharp.
Stay sharp.

That's the Standard.

26. Don't Meet without a Mission

Lesson: Meetings cost time. Make them count.

Nothing kills momentum like a meeting with no point.

People talk in circles.
Buzzwords fly.
No agenda. No decisions. Just noise.

If you're leading a team, you don't let that slide.

If people are in the room, they're there to move.

So when a meeting starts drifting, stop it on the spot.

Ask one question:

"What's the goal of this meeting?"

If no one can answer it clearly, it ends.

No dragging it out. No pretending it's productive.

If it's not useful, it's over.

Because meetings aren't free.

- They cost time.
- They cost focus.
- They cost energy that should've gone to actual work.

And most of the time?

Doing the work beats talking about it.

So if the meeting's not ready, cancel it.

- If it's off-track, reset it.
- If it's just noise, shut it down.

Come back with purpose.

Come back when it matters.

- No filler.
- No theater.
- **Just clear, useful time.**

That's not formality.

That's discipline.

27. Stop Trying to Be Liked

Lesson: Leadership is clarity, not people-pleasing.

You might be sharp.

You might have presence.

You might even have people's respect.

But if you're still hesitating to set the tone because you want to be liked, then you're not leading yet.

- You're managing feelings.
- You're avoiding conflict.
- You're choosing comfort over clarity.

And when that happens, the Standard slips.

Because leadership doesn't require volume.

It requires edge.

Not aggression. Not ego.
Just edge rooted in fairness.

If you want respect, model it.
If you want trust, earn it.
If you want alignment, carry it.

And if you want to lead? Stop worrying about being liked.

That means:

- Holding the line, even when it's unpopular
- Protecting the Standard without flinching
- Cutting favoritism
- Delivering accountability; calm, clean, and consistent

You don't have to be loud.

But you do have to be clear.

You don't have to be tough.

But you do have to be honest.

The ones who are ready will follow that.

They'll respect it.

They'll grow under it.

And the ones who can't?

They're not ready to lead.

Not yet.

28. The Senior Leader Who Won't Evolve

Lesson: Progress doesn't wait for pride.

You'll face this eventually.

Someone who helped build the foundation,

Who's been around. Who's earned trust.

But now they're stuck.

- They resist change.
- They dismiss new ideas.
- They slow things down, not by what they do, but by what they refuse to do.

And you can't ignore it.

But you also don't need a showdown.

This isn't about ego. It's about direction.

Because progress doesn't pause for seniority.

And it doesn't ask permission from the past.
You can respect what someone has built—

Without letting them block what's next.

So you move.

- Not with noise.
- Not with force.
- Just calm, clear, decisive direction.

You don't fight them.

You don't drag them.

You just stop waiting.

Because strong teams don't get trapped in history.

They learn from it and then they keep going.

- No drama.
- No apology.
- Just forward.

29. When Kindness Becomes Neglect

Lesson: Silence isn't neutral, it's permission.

I've lived this one, more than once.

But not anymore.

There were people on my team I should've let go.

Not because they were failing technically
but because they were **exploiters.**

They didn't carry the Custodian mindset.

They weren't aligned with the mission.
They looked out for themselves and quietly drained the team.

And I waited too long.

- Out of kindness, I stalled.
- Out of loyalty, I tolerated.
- Out of fear of conflict, I kept letting it slide.

I told myself I was being steady. Supportive.

But the truth?

I was avoiding the hard call.

And it cost us.

- Top performers pulled back.
- The culture softened.
- Momentum slipped.

Because my silence wasn't neutral—it was permission.

And when you're the leader, your permission shapes everything. That's when I got clear.

Now, when I see it, when someone doesn't carry the Standard, doesn't live the mindset, doesn't belong in the mission:

- I don't hesitate.
- I remove them from my presence.
- I protect the team.
- I protect the work.

No drama. No emotion. Just clarity.

Because leadership isn't about being harsh.

But it is about being honest.

Silence isn't kindness. It's permission.
And I don't give that kind of permission anymore

SECTION 5: FUTURE-PROOFING THE MISSION

30. Promotions Aren't Just About Readiness

Lesson: Influence in the wrong hands erodes trust.

I've promoted people who weren't ready.

- Some of them had the experience.
- Some had the time served.
- Some looked perfect on paper.

But when it came time to carry people, not just tasks they couldn't do it.

Not because they were bad people.

But because leadership requires more than competence.

- It demands presence.
- It demands emotional control.
- It demands trust.

I've seen the Peter Principle in action, people getting promoted until they hit the wall they can't climb.

It's not fair to them.

And it's not fair to the team.

Just because someone's technically "ready" doesn't mean they're the right fit for the role.

- If the role is highly technical, execution-heavy, process-driven, maybe they can grow into it.
- Maybe you can build the structure around them.

Coach them. Stretch them. Support them as they level up.

But if the role involves people?

- If it sets tone
- Carries culture
- Affects trust across the team

That's not the place to experiment.

Because influence in the wrong hands does more than hurt results.

- It erodes trust.
- It drives good people away.
- It confuses the Standard.

So now, I take a harder look.

I still grow people.

I still promote from within.

But I don't confuse loyalty with readiness.

And I don't confuse time served with leadership.

- I coach first.
- Stretch second.
- And promote only when both are locked in.

Because I'm not interested in just filling seats.

I'm building leaders who can carry real weight.

31. The Unexpected Vacancy

Lesson: Build continuity before the seat's empty.

One day the person in that critical role just won't be there.

- No warning.
- No handoff.

- Just an empty chair at the worst possible time.

It happens.

And when it does, teams that planned are steady.

Teams that didn't? They scramble.

You can't build continuity in a crisis.

You build it in advance.

- Every critical role should have a second in line.
- Someone cross-trained. Someone trusted.
- Not just someone available but someone capable.

If that plan doesn't exist?

You carry the weight carefully until it does.

Not with panic. With discipline.

You don't promote just to fill the gap.

You don't lower the Standard just because someone's missing.

You hold the line.
You protect the mission.
And you prepare better next time.

Because leadership isn't just about who's sitting in the seat.

It's about whether the mission keeps moving, even if they're not.

32. Learn Both Sides of the Work

Lesson: When teams speak different languages translate both languages to align teams.

In every operation, there's a gap.

- There's the team under pressure; building, solving, moving.

- And there's the team supporting them from a distance; planning, managing, processing.

One side says, *"They don't get it."*

The other says, *"They don't follow the system."*

They're both right if no one's bridging the gap.

That's your job.

If you lead people, manage workflows, or write policy:

You need to understand what it feels like to execute under fire.

Because:

- The front line doesn't have time for perfect plans.
- They won't follow what they don't trust.
- And support can't help what it doesn't understand.

You need to speak both languages.

- Technical and practical.
- Field and office.
- Execution and process.

Don't hide behind forms and protocol.

Don't talk down to the people doing the work.

And don't expect perfect compliance from people you've never walked with.

Lead the work by knowing the work.

Walk both sides.
Listen closely.
Translate clearly.

**That's how you keep teams aligned.
And that's how the work actually gets done.**

33. Fast Isn't Always Forward

Lesson: Leadership is how long you can carry the weight.

You're sharp.
You've got ideas.
You want to prove yourself and fast.

That's not the problem.
The problem is pace.

You start sprinting.
- You bring the energy, the drive, the noise.
- But if you're not careful, what feels like momentum turns into friction.

People feel stepped over.

- Context gets skipped.
- The pace of the team gets out of sync and now your speed is working against you.

Strong teams don't kill urgency.
They **channel** it.

If you're moving too fast, too soon, the answer isn't to slow down just to fit in:

It's to build trust before you try to move the system.

You might be ready to go.

- But leadership isn't about how fast you can prove it.
- It's about how long you can carry it.

So learn the terrain.

Earn your footing.

Take the time to understand the people, the structure, the work.

Because without that foundation, your speed won't scale.

- It'll burn out.
- Or worse, burn bridges.

Fast doesn't mean forward.
Steady does.

34. When the System Says No

Lesson: Always hold your ground for a fair chance.

I was 17 years old when the system told me no.

- I had applied to Texas A&M University.
- My dream school, my goal, the only option I gave myself.

It was the only school I applied to. Because in all honesty, I couldn't afford the cost of multiple applications.

As I mentioned in the Prologue, I wasn't born in this country.

- English isn't my first language.
- And while my math and science scores were top tier, my reading score dragged me down.

On paper, I didn't qualify. So they rejected me.

Most people would've accepted it. I didn't.

I put on my best clothes, drove to the university, and walked into the admissions office.

- When the front desk told me the counselors were too busy, I sat down and waited.
- When they offered me an appointment that was weeks out, I simply said, "No." And that I wasn't leaving.

I didn't raise my voice. I didn't beg. I just said clearly:

"I'm not leaving until someone looks me in the eye."

Eventually, someone did.

I told them:

"Don't just look at the total score. Break it down. I've been working on my English, and I'll keep going.

"But I didn't apply to teach it, I applied to study engineering."

I didn't ask for favors.
I asked for a shot.

Give me a probation period. Let me prove I belong.

- If I failed, I'd leave.
- If I passed, I'd keep going.

They didn't promise anything. But a few weeks later, I got the letter:

Provisional admission. Summer start. High bar.

I hit it.
And then some.

I graduated from that school.

- Built my life.
- Built my company.
- And I never forgot that moment.

Sometimes the system says no, not because you're wrong, but because it didn't take the time to see what's in front of it.

So when the gate is locked, and the people behind the desk tell you, "Not yet,"

You don't throw a fit. You don't walk away quiet.

> *You sit.*
> *You wait.*
> *You ask again.*

And when the door opens, you make the ask that matters.

- Not for a free pass.
- For a fair chance.

That's what separates the ones who wait to be chosen—
from the ones who make it undeniable.

CHAPTER NINE

Hold the Line, No Way But Through

IF YOU CHOOSE TO LIVE BY A CODE LIKE THIS, EXPECT TO BE MISUNDERSTOOD.

People won't know where to place you.

You won't fit the mold. You won't follow trends.
You'll make some uncomfortable just by being consistent.

Some will say you're too intense.

- Too serious.
- Too direct.
- Others will call you loyal, honest, fair.

Some will call you difficult.

- Hard to read.
- Even intimidating.

You'll hear both and both will be true in their own way.

Some will question your choices.

- Why you don't dress to impress.
- Why you walk in with quiet confidence, like you don't need anyone's approval.

And when you do decide to show out, you'll do it on your terms and they'll feel it.

Some companies will try to copy you.
Some people will try to outwork you.
Others will just try to figure out what makes you different.

And the truth is, they won't get it at first.

- They'll say you have a branding problem.
- That you should smile more. Be more marketable. Play along.

But **you're not playing games,** you're building something real.

Some will criticize you in private. Others will praise you quietly *because they know you wouldn't accept the compliment anyway.*

- Not because you're cold.
- But because you know the race isn't over.
- You don't care who's ahead or behind.

You're just running your race with your eyes forward.

You won't be liked by everyone
and if you are, you're probably doing it wrong.

Some will say, *"There's no way someone like that is real."*

But then the years go by.
You don't change. You don't fold. You don't fake it.

And eventually even the doubters start to respect it.

Because deep down, they know:

- You're not like the rest.
- You're not trying to be.
- You're just different in every way that matters.

And that's what the Custodian Code does.

It won't make you liked by everyone.
It won't make you the loudest or the most celebrated.
But it will make you stand out,
not because you were trying to…

But because you never needed to fit in.

You made it.

Not just through the pages;

But through

- Every excuse
- Every doubt
- Every voice that told you to coast.

Now the real work begins.

Because this isn't a book you finish.

It's a Standard you carry.

A Code that doesn't live on paper; it lives under pressure.

When things go sideways.
When the shortcut shows up.
When no one's watching.

That's when it counts.
That's when you hold the line.

- Not for applause.
- Not for a title.
- But because you said you would.

And in a world full of noise, shortcuts, and hollow leadership,
you didn't just read the difference.

You *became* it.

Leadership isn't loud.

It's not polished.

It's not perfect.

It's the quiet resolve to do what's right, when it would be easier not to.

- It's owning your decisions.
- Protecting your people.
- Finishing the job clean.

You don't need permission to do that.

- You just need clarity.
- Conviction.
- And the will to carry something heavier than yourself.

Because there's no way around this work.
No cheat code for real leadership.
No shortcut to legacy.

There's only one way forward:

No way but through

So here's your charge:

- Hold the line when it shakes.
- Lead when it's inconvenient.
- Protect what you've built, before it breaks.
- And when it gets hard?

Don't flinch. Don't coast. Don't quit.

Rest if you must. Reset if you have to.
Then come back sharper.

You didn't make it this far to start letting things slide.
You came to build something that lasts.

And one day, when someone says:

"They did it right."

You'll know why it mattered.

Because the ones who make impact?

They didn't fake the work.
They didn't play the game.
They held the line.
And they led the only way that counts—

Through.

Final line:

Be the one who holds the line, **because there's no way but through.**

That's the Standard. Now go carry it.

What Holds Under Pressure

In this segment I added what a call a vault of truths: tested, carried, and clarified through real weight.

These aren't summaries. These are anchors.

Come back to them when the Standard slips.

When it gets loud.

When it gets fast.

When it's tempting to shortcut the work.

Because this is what holds.

LEADERSHIP

- Build leaders, not dependents.
- Carry the weight. Without edits.
- Clarity doesn't mean saying everything. It means saying only what the moment can carry.
- Excellence doesn't always need a title. But it always needs proof.
- Leadership contains urgency, it doesn't spread it.
- Leadership doesn't require noise. It requires weight.
- Leadership doesn't start when you step away. It starts the moment you build someone who can carry part of the weight without you.
- Leadership isn't earned in ease. It's revealed under weight.
- Real leadership shows up when it hurts.
- You don't lead through convenience. You lead through conviction.
- You don't need a title to carry weight. You need a Standard that holds.

INTEGRITY

- If my name is on it, it has to be right.
- Integrity doesn't run in one direction. It holds even when no one is watching.
- Integrity isn't a moment. It's a rhythm.
- Protect the Standard on both sides of the deal.
- Protecting the Standard means calling it, owning it, and fixing it.
- Respect is the floor. Integrity is non-negotiable.
- Standards don't get tested when everything is running smooth. They get tested when something breaks.
- Stewardship isn't a role. It's a vow.
- Uniform Standard, customized delivery
- What you tolerate becomes the Standard.
- You don't fix drift by adding noise. You fix it by returning to the Standard.

CULTURE

- A team doesn't break when it fails. It breaks when it lets failure slide.
- A team is only as strong as its weakest habits.
- Do not trade long-term trust for short-term motion.
- Influence in the wrong hands erodes trust.
- Ownership of one mistake creates oxygen for the team.
- Politics is a tax strong teams don't pay.
- Strong rooms don't stay calm by accident. Someone protects the tone.
- The sharpest cultures fail when weak habits are left unchallenged.
- What you tolerate becomes the new normal.
- When Teams speak different languages translate both languages to align teams.
- You don't build trust with policies. You build it with presence.

COMMUNICATION

- Cash gives you space. Space gives you clarity.
- Clarity comes from decision, not drama.
- Clarity fixes more than blame ever will.
- Don't confuse silence for steadiness. Sometimes it's corrosion.
- Quitting doesn't start loud. It starts with silence and slow detachment.
- Silence doesn't protect people. It blindsides them.
- Silence is not always wrong. But it is never neutral.
- Silence isn't discipline; sometimes it's a warning.
- Silence isn't neutral, it's permission.

DISCIPLINE

- Discipline is not rigidity. It's timing, awareness, and control.
- Excuses get easier every time. Don't start.
- Real decisions deserve discipline, not speed.

TEAMWORK

- Build continuity before the seat's empty.
- Build the bench before the storm hits.
- Heart can't be taught. Skill can.
- Loyalty is a two-way street.

GROWTH

- Always hold your ground for a fair chance.
- Burnout is not a badge. It's a warning.
- Compassion is not weakness. It is the refusal to win by devaluing others.
- Conviction is not volume. It is the refusal to hide.
- Distractions don't just slow you down. They drain the system and make you think you're making progress.

- Don't call it momentum if it's just motion with no return.
- Emotion is not a strategy.
- If the return isn't there, stop pretending it will be.
- If you lose the how, the win doesn't matter.
- If you would hide it, don't do it.
- Just because something is moving doesn't mean it's building.
- Know when to push and when to walk.
- Meetings cost time. Make them count.
- More isn't better. Better is better.
- No way around. No way back. No way but through.
- No win is worth it if it costs what matters most.
- People don't follow speeches. They follow steadiness.
- Performance without character is a time bomb.
- Progress doesn't wait for pride.
- Shortcuts don't always show up dirty. They show up disguised as efficiency.
- Shortcuts don't stay in their lane. They bleed into other lanes.
- Speed blurs. Slowing down clarifies.
- The mission is bigger than me. Humility keeps it that way.
- The moment you trade your uniqueness, what's left isn't you. It's a version built to please.
- The process is the real prize.
- You don't get more time. You get sharper.
- You don't rise to the occasion. You sink to the level of your preparation.

STRATEGY & SYSTEMS

- If it doesn't serve the mission, it doesn't deserve the investment.
- Systems don't collapse from pressure. They collapse from erosion.
- Turning down bad work is an excellent strategy. Fear is a bad strategy.
- You don't get more space. You protect the space you already have.
- Momentum without direction is just movement.

Examples of
What the Custodian Creed
Looks Like in Real Life

IF YOU ARE A PARENT:

I do not exist to be seen.

I don't parent for applause or attention. I show up even when no one notices.

I exist to protect what matters.

I guard my child's safety, peace, and future even when it's inconvenient.

I move not for applause, but for duty.

I do what's needed, not what's noticed.

I build what will outlive me, even if no one remembers my name.

I pass down values, not just comfort. I focus on who they become, not how they make me look.

I trust the mission more than I trust my fears.

I don't let anxiety or self-doubt dictate how I raise my child. I act with purpose.

I choose the discipline of action over the comfort of excuses.

I lean in when it's hard. I don't default to "not now" when presence is needed.

I understand that shortcuts only delay the debt that must one day be paid.

I stay consistent. I don't cut corners on attention, correction, or love.

I do not measure my worth by recognition.

I don't need praise to know I'm parenting well.

I measure it by the quiet, lasting positive impact on the lives I touch.

If my child becomes grounded, kind, and steady; that is enough.

I accept that I may never see the harvest.

I plant what they may not understand until long after I'm gone.

I accept that my work may be forgotten.

They may not remember the sacrifices. That doesn't change their value.

I accept that the world may still fall after I am gone.

I give them strength anyway.

But while I am here I will fight. I will build. I will serve. I will protect.

That is what parenting asks. And I accept.

Because the work itself is the reward.

The growth. The grounding. The love. That's enough.

Because stewardship is the only true inheritance.

I pass down responsibility, not entitlement.

There is no way around. There is no way back. There is only the way through.

I stay in it; even on the hard days.

I am a Custodian. And I endure.

Because they need me to.

IF YOU ARE A SMALL BUSINESS OWNER:

I do not exist to be seen.

I don't build for social status. I build to provide and protect.

I exist to protect what matters.

I protect my people, my values, and the work I've promised to deliver.

I move not for applause, but for duty.

I show up and carry what no one else sees.

I build what will outlive me, even if no one remembers my name.

I create something worth inheriting; even if I never see it scale.

I trust the mission more than I trust my fears.

I bet on the work. I bet on the team. I bet on the Standard.

I choose the discipline of action over the comfort of excuses.

There's no one to blame. I move forward anyway.

I understand that shortcuts only delay the debt that must one day be paid.

I do it right, even when it costs more, takes longer, or hurts more.

I do not measure my worth by recognition.

No one sees what it takes. I still carry the weight.

I measure it by the quiet, lasting positive impact on the lives I touch.

If someone grows here, if one family eats because of this, then it's worth it.

I accept that I may never see the harvest.
   I still plant. I still build. I still give my best.

I accept that my work may be forgotten.
   Legacy isn't about being remembered. It's about building right.

I accept that the world may still fall after I am gone.
   I can't control the outcome. I control my effort.

But while I am here, I will fight. I will build. I will serve. I will protect.
   That's what leadership means to me.

Because the work itself is the reward.
   Every job done right. Every person protected.

Because stewardship is the only true inheritance.
   I don't just own this. I hold it for those who come next.

There is no way around. There is no way back. There is only the way through.
   So I keep going. Especially when it's hard.

I am a Custodian. And I endure.
   Because this is mine to carry.

IF YOU ARE AN EDUCATOR:

I do not exist to be seen.
   I don't teach for praise, attention, or performance. I teach because shaping minds is sacred.

I exist to protect what matters.
   I protect dignity, curiosity, and the quiet confidence of students who are still becoming.

I move not for applause, but for duty.
   I show up when I'm tired. I stay steady when others drift.

I build what will outlive me, even if no one remembers my name.

My lessons live in decisions made long after the classroom is gone.

I trust the mission more than I trust my fears.

I speak truth even when it's unpopular. I stay grounded when systems shift.

I choose the discipline of action over the comfort of excuses.

I adapt. I create. I do not quit when it gets messy.

I understand that shortcuts only delay the debt that must one day be paid.

I don't lower the Standard. I bring people up to meet it.

I do not measure my worth by recognition.

My name may not be remembered. My impact will be.

I measure it by the quiet, lasting positive impact on the lives I touch.

If one student thinks more clearly or walks more confidently because of me, that's enough.

I accept that I may never see the harvest.

The seeds I plant may not bloom for years. I still plant.

I accept that my work may be forgotten.

That doesn't lessen the value of the effort.

I accept that the world may still fall after I am gone.

I teach anyway. I give them what they'll need to carry weight I will never see.

But while I am here I will fight. I will build. I will serve. I will protect.

That is the calling. That is the Code.

Because the work itself is the reward.

The process of shaping someone else's strength is worth everything.

Because stewardship is the only true inheritance.

I give them not just facts, but judgment, clarity, and courage.

There is no way around. There is no way back. There is only the way through.

So I stay in it. Especially when it's hard.

I am a Custodian. And I endure.

Because they deserve someone who does.

The **Custodian Creed** is not tied to a title.

It belongs to anyone who carries the weight with discipline and without noise.

It can be lived in any role, in any season, by anyone who chooses to protect what matters.

If the work is real, the Creed applies.

If the weight is yours, the words will hold.

You don't need permission to carry it.

Just the courage to mean it.

Below is the Daily Custodian Affirmation. Carry it into your mornings. Repeat it when the Standard feels heavy. Let it remind you what kind of weight you were built to hold.

Custodian Affirmation

I am not here to be seen.

I am here to protect what matters.

I trust the mission more than I trust my fear.

I move with depth, not haste.

I lift, I build, I serve, no matter who notices.

The work is bigger than me.

And because of that, I will endure beyond me.

No way around.

No way back.

No way but THROUGH

About the Author

Amjad Jaber didn't build a career on giving professional advice.

He helped build a real company, from nothing,
by choosing people who believed in the Standard,
protecting them, and carrying the weight alongside them.

He didn't do it alone.

He chose well.

And together, they built something strong enough to matter and
hold even when everything around them tried to erode it.

He wrote this book not to shine a light on himself,
*but to **pass forward the Code and the Standard***
that held when everything else tried to pull it apart.

*This is not a book about perfection, **it is a message.***

*A quiet stand for what is **good,** against what is broken.*

He hopes it reminds someone that the weight is worth it
and they are not alone in carrying it.